Praises For:

Finding God, Finding Me

Izzy Koo won me over with her candid confession, "I honestly didn't know why I was a Christian." From there, she writes a powerful testimony of encountering God that changed everything from her identity and confidence to purpose and passion. The result is a book that offers hope to the battles that every teenager faces: loneliness, emptiness, depression, anxiety, and bitterness. The impact of Izzy's testimony is profound—it resonates not only with Christians but also with seekers and skeptics—and encourages all to look to Jesus for solutions that the world cannot offer. *Finding God, Finding Me* is so personal and introspective, and I highly recommend parents to give this book to their children who might be struggling spiritually.

Izzy's testimony addresses teens right where they are and encourages them to experience the transforming power of God's love.

—**Michael Lee**, Senior Pastor of *All Nations Community Church*.

**

Izzy Koo's ***Finding God, Finding Me***, would have to be one of the most inspiring testimonies I've ever heard of. This book proves how real our God is. The moments in Izzy's life are ones that all youth can relate to and find courage in the challenging seasons of life. Izzy demonstrates her triumphs as well as her battles that let the reader know that they aren't alone, and have a God who gives us victory. The boldness, the passion to serve our King and others, the hunger, the love, the kindness, and care she gives, has inspired me and will keep inspiring others to seek the Lord diligently. Because I want what Izzy's on! Izzy has majorly influenced my confidence to know who I am in Christ and you can see how the Lord uses her and speaks through her throughout this whole book.

I hope this book blesses and touches you as much as it did to me. All Glory be to God, and I'm so proud of you Izzy, for being a willing vessel to be used.

—**Sarah Daniela Ortega**, MFDV Youth and Worship Leader.

**

I wish I had read ***Finding God, Finding Me*** back when I was in middle school, trying to figure out my faith for myself and what it meant to me. The way this book is broken up into sections of different qualities Izzy had discovered about herself through her God-given experiences is incredibly digestible for readers, young and old, who want to dive deeper into their relationship with God. I am usually not one to finish a book from start to finish in one sitting, but it felt as though I was reading through a diary of Izzy's life or having a mentor speak to me through conversation. It blows my mind that while God calls the most seasoned pastors to spread His word, He also uses mere *teenagers* to further His kingdom using the gifts He's blessed them with. *Finding God, Finding Me* is a beautiful testament to that truth, and I am confident that Izzy's writing will have the most eye-opening impact on those who get their hands on this book.

—**Yuna Song**, Senior at *Bellevue High School.*

***

Where do I even begin? I can't even start to explain how proud I am of my sister. All my life she has been my sister, best friend, and inspiration, and seeing her write this book and living her life to glorify God has been so amazing. I have seen in person how God has changed her, and I'm so amazed and inspired that God can truly make a person new again. Reading this book, I am positive that other kids and teens my age will be so inspired to seek God and find their identity in him.

—**Olivia Koo**, Izzy's little sister (11 years old).

Finding God, Finding Me, is ultimately a journey and guide to self. It offers you deep and personal revelations that Izzy imparts to her readers. This is an offering and invitation for readers, of any age, to gain a better understanding of purpose, by coming into a closer relationship with the creator and giver of it. Whether you believe in God, consider yourself to be a Christian, or not, Izzy provides a fresh and relatable approach to understanding identity, offering strategies on how to navigate our everyday human emotions and struggles.

Through vulnerability and generosity, Izzy proves and reminds us that God doesn't call the qualified, but he qualifies the called. Izzy lives by one of her favorite verses - 1 Timothy 4:12 which says, "Don't let anyone look down on you because you are young, but set an example for the believers in speech, in conduct, in love, in faith, and purity." *Finding God, Finding Me* is a MUST read! It has provided clarity and direction for my personal life and journey!

—**Derek Jackson**, Actor and Activist.

Finding God, Finding Me

How I met God as an ordinary teenager

IZZY KOO

Published by KHARIS PUBLISHING, imprint of KHARIS MEDIA LLC.

Copyright © 2021 Izzy Koo

ISBN-13: 978-1-63746-030-6

ISBN-10: 1-63746-030-9

Library of Congress Control Number: 2021934510

All KHARIS PUBLISHING products are available at special quantity discounts for bulk purchase for sales promotions, premiums, fund-raising, and educational needs. For details, contact:

Kharis Media LLC

Tel: 1-479-599-8657

support@kharispublishing.com

www.kharispublishing.com

This book is dedicated to all the teenagers out there who are searching.

Table of contents

Foreword

I remember the first time Izzy reached out to me with a simple text of gratitude after my first youth retreat as her pastor. Little did she know, she was one of the first students to initiate a relationship with me, something I held so preciously before God. Because to God it's all about the *one*. As we met up for the first time across from one another, her questions and her undivided attention towards me, moved me. This girl was so curious and devoted. As I began to redirect the questions towards her and her story, I saw a young teenager who was capable, strong, loving and giving of herself. I wondered. *What is your dream, Izzy? What do you think your purpose is?* As cheesy and bold these questions are,

I love asking such questions in the most mundane of circumstances, because I love to see how the other person responds. It was in that moment Izzy's answer blew me away. I saw her beating and desperate heart for her generation. I saw *God's heart* in her.

Moments like this is what uncovers the hidden mystery of God's glory in each of us. It is innate in us, *his heart* in us. There are no small people in God's eyes, no small gift. "Every good and every perfect gift is from above, coming down from the Father of lights, with whom there is no variation or shadow due to change." James 1:17.

I hope for you as the reader, whoever you are, may not just read this book, but receive this book. Receive what it stirs up for you. Receive the hope it brings. Receive the longings it stirs in you. Hope is never far from each of us. Empowerment is always personal. The hope you long to see in yourself is possible, because you and I were made by a God who restores his true Image in all of us. Let Him.

—Esther Youn Chung.

Introduction

Hey guys! My name is Izzy, and I'm just an ordinary high school student (currently in my sophomore year). Honestly, there's nothing extraordinary about me. I walk down the halls of school every weekday and stay up late doing homework every night. I'm your typical table partner, someone you would introduce yourself to on your first day of school, and someone you might brush shoulders against as you walk to class. I'm no class president or even a sports team captain—I'm just another kid at school who is trying to graduate like everyone else.

My "ordinary-ness" might be a little shocking, considering that you are holding a book about my life in your hands; usually, people who write books about their lives are anything but typical and ordinary. I mean, with Christian books, you're probably used to reading books by authors with high credibility and credentials. I know I am. I've read so many books of faith over the years, all by incredible authors who inspire me, and I look up to them as my role models. These authors are people with a wealth of knowledge and decades of experience. Some are famous preachers, non-profit organizations starters, former professional athletes, or well-known celebrities. (Spoiler alert: If you didn't notice this already, I am none of these things. Not even close.)

But the fact I am just an ordinary sixteen-year-old girl is exactly why I wanted to write this book, because *even though* I'm not famous or well-known, God still met me where I was, and radically changed my life. Despite having no special qualifications to write, and not being an exceptional writer, I have a story *about a transformational God* that I know I have to share. And believe me, I struggled so much with writing one English paper at school that I would *not* have written a whole book about my God and how I met Him, if it wasn't the most amazing, life-altering experience in the entire world.

With all that said, this book is my testimony of how I found God and how He has radically changed my life. I went from being a shy, closed-off, and insecure teenager to completely finding myself in God and becoming a confident, passionate follower of Christ. In the following pages, you will read about the experiences that have shaped me, the obstacles I have overcome, but most importantly, you'll read about the greatness of God.

He has changed and filled me in ways that nothing else ever could, and I know He can change you in the same ways if you let Him. I pray that as you read my story, God will take you on a journey that leads you to the happiness, genuine joy, and incredible peace I have found on my own journey with Him.

Even if you're reading this and thinking, *I don't really believe in God*, this book is still for you! I started the same way; I didn't start out madly in love with Jesus. In fact, I started off quite the opposite. Although I grew up in a Christian home, I didn't believe the faith for myself. I thought Christianity was just a go-to-church-on-Sundays-and-read-the-Bible-sometimes thing. I didn't realize Christianity was so much more than that.

God isn't someone we just learn or read about. He is Someone with whom we can have an actual *relationship*. He is the source of all love, joy, and peace. He is the only way out of the dangerous cycle of loneliness, anxiety, and depression to which we all fall victim at some point in our lives. And do you know what the most amazing part is? It's that God doesn't require anything from you; He accepts you as you are. In fact, God *loves* you as you are. He longs to have a relationship with you and He has already forgiven whatever wrongs you have done in the past.

God has a life of fullness and joy prepared for you. I have experienced what it's like to receive new life in Jesus, and my hope is that this book will help you find your life in Him as well. I know each of you who are reading this is coming in with your unique personal story, your specific struggles, and your adversaries, but in these pages, I will introduce you to a God who will meet you wherever you are.

God isn't just for some people. He's not just for the pastors and missionaries, nor only for people with power or status. He's not just for people who have it all together, who seem perfect, or who even grew up in the faith. No, God is for people who are broken, deeply drowned in shame and guilt; He is for the ordinary, the typical, the young, inexperienced, and unqualified. God is for everyone. God is for teenagers. God is for *you*!

I encourage you to read this book as if it's your best friend telling you how they met Jesus, not a preacher or pastor, but a teenager just like you. I didn't write this book as an instruction manual or a book of tips and advice. I wrote it as if I were sitting across from you at a coffee shop and simply sharing my story with you. Raw. Vulnerable. Real.

At the beginning of each chapter there is a question, and each question is one I have been asked—sometimes even at a coffee shop with a friend! My answers to these questions have encouraged others to get to know this Jesus I have the privilege of knowing. So, as I answer these questions in more depth through each chapter, I hope and pray you will be inspired to seek Jesus in your life as well.

From one teenager to another, I'm telling you that you can only find everything you are searching for in this world in Jesus—identity, confidence, patience, passion, purpose, humility, and most important, *yourself.* You can find all that in God and God alone.

That's why this book is called *Finding God, Finding Me.* It's because the moment you find God and allow Him to change your life, you will not only find things like your identity and confidence, but you'll also find yourself in the process. People spend a lifetime trying to discover who they are and what their life's purpose is. I believe with all my heart that you can only find those things in God. So, without further ado, this is the story of *finding me.*

1

Finding God

"Hey Izzy, how did you find God?"

It's a crazy story, really. I was just a typical kid in high school like you. I was an introvert, a volleyball addict, and an average student. I was an impatient sister, a teenager who thought she was always right, and a big ball of insecurity. I was closed-off, scared to death of public speaking, and never raised my hand in class. Oh! And I was also a Christian. Well, maybe more like a half-Christian. Let me tell you what I mean.

Growing up in the church, I knew all the popular Bible stories. You probably know which ones I'm talking about. Yup, from Adam and Eve, to Jonah and the big fish, all the way to Jesus dying on the cross, these stories were ingrained in my memory. I was that Sunday school kid raising her hand to every question because I had memorized every answer (Actually, no... I was too shy to raise my hand, *but* I always knew the answer in my head. That's what counts, right?). As I sat on the carpeted floor of the Sunday school classroom, I would excitedly anticipate when the pastor would ask a question I knew the answer to. When I knew the answer, I prided myself that I sounded so "Christian-y."

But as I got older, these questions and stories became so routine that I realized I didn't have any real faith behind all those memorized answers. It was like all the science tests I took at school. I had all the formulas and vocabulary memorized like the back of my hand, but if you had asked me to explain why a particular reaction worked, or why a certain process led to this or that outcome, I would've looked at you with a blank stare. I would have had no idea. I don't know whether that was just a middle school thing or a "me" thing, but I was just into memorizing information—not actually understanding or applying it. Likewise, with church, I soon realized I didn't have any reasoning or conviction that grounded anything I was saying. Everything became so familiar that these stories that were supposed to be incredible and amazing, seemed like any other vocabulary flashcard. They had lost all their power and significance.

For me, church just became a place where I would catch up with my friends and hear some good worship music. I never saw it as a place I went for God. Instead, I would constantly think things like, *I hope I see that cute guy today*, or, *I hope service ends early so I can go meet my friends afterward*. Every Sunday, as I sat listening to message after message, everything my pastors said sounded like broken records. Yes, I knew God loved me. And yes, I knew Jesus died for me, but did I truly understand the *magnitude* of that? I'd say I definitely didn't.

Why are you Christian?

I remember one Sunday, my dad and I were eating dinner together, and he asked me about what I learned at church that morning. As usual, my brain frantically tried to remember my pastor's message. I probably rambled off something completely unrelated to anything my pastor actually talked about because, frankly, I didn't really pay much attention during services. I found them boring, repetitive, and useless when trying to apply them to my life. Still, every week without fail, my dad would ask me what I learned, so sometimes I tried to pay attention just so I could answer the questions I knew he would ask me.

That Sunday, my answer must have been really bad because my dad paused. He then proceeded to ask me a question I would soon realize is incredibly difficult for any "half-Christian" to answer. He looked at me and asked, "Izzy, why are *you* Christian?" I remember just sitting in my chair, trying to come up with a good answer. I kept thinking, *C'mon Izzy, why are you Christian? You've been a "Christian" for what, fifteen years? Tell Dad why you're a Christian!* But as I kept searching for the answer to what I thought was a fairly simple question, I realized I couldn't find it. I honestly didn't know why I was a Christian. I knew what Christians were supposed to do and know, but I didn't understand why I was one in the first place. Flushed with embarrassment, I finally looked up at my dad and grudgingly confessed, "I don't know, Dad."

I was stumped. It wasn't a question I could answer by saying something like, "Because that's just how I grew up," or, "Because *you're* a Christian, Dad." I knew this question was much deeper than that. My dad was asking why *I* was a Christian and why *I* believed everything I claimed to believe. But the truth was, I had never really thought about it. My whole life, I had always been so sure I was a Christian, but now I wasn't so sure. The only thing I was sure about was that this question wouldn't leave my head. For the first time, it made me wonder whether my faith was real, or if it had always just been a label I put on. I began to doubt whether I ever genuinely believed it for *myself*.

Faith put to the test
Until my eighth-grade year, I never questioned my faith. But after hearing my dad's question, I started thinking twice about everything I had ever believed. I carried this doubt into my first year of high school.

As I began that year, I noticed right away that the high school I was attending was extremely secular. Not many people were religious, and even if they were, no one talked about it. It wasn't like the middle school I went to, where kids spoke about their faith and religion all the time. Back in those days, talking freely and openly about those kinds of things had been completely normal.

Not in high school. Apparently, religion was not something to talk about. That worried me. I didn't want to be that *one* Christian when no one else was. But I also didn't want to just ditch my faith. I knew it was important to my family that I stood firm in it. So, in a place of guilt for not wanting to abandon my faith completely, I decided to be somewhat open about it, at least to my close friends. I mean, *what was the worst that could happen?*

Going into my freshman year, I had a tight group of friends that had been with me since middle school. We were so tight, in fact, that I never thought to branch out. This friend group was all I thought I needed, so I had the mindset that I wouldn't necessarily reach out to any new people or build any new friendships. I was shy and pretty closed-off to new people anyway, so I figured, *why branch out if I already have a solid friend group, right?* Plus, two of the four friends were Christians. And while the other two were atheists, they were super open people and didn't mind our faith. It seemed like I was all set. I couldn't ask for a better friend group.

In our conversations with each other, my two Christian friends and I would talk about our churches and youth groups. We would even invite each other to visit our churches. None of us were super passionate about

5

Christianity or anything, but we liked that we had it in common. Even the other two would come to church with us sometimes, just to see what it was like.

During the middle of the year, however, I saw a shift in all my friends' attitudes toward Christianity. It happened suddenly, so I was curious to see how church was going for my two Christian friends. During lunch one day, I asked them about it and was surprised to find out they had both stopped going to church. Not only had they stopped going, but they also seemed to be against the whole idea of the religion itself. I knew something was up when I also noticed my two atheist friends were suddenly a lot more heavily atheistic than I remembered. I was so confused. I had no idea why everyone had such a dramatic, sudden behavior change. But since it was so random and unlike my friends to change so abruptly, I figured it wasn't too big of a deal and continued to interact with them the same way I always had.

But things were different. A few days after their behavior change, my friends and I were hanging out at one of our houses. We sat on my friend's couch, laughed, and talked about the usual things best friends laugh and talk about, but after about an hour of that, one of my friends brought up a political and slightly controversial topic. My friends loved politics, so we would often debate current issues and everyone stated their stance on the topic at hand. I did not like having these debates because, frankly, I never knew what my friends were talking about (Who can relate?). Luckily, some topics were things I learned about in church, so whenever it was my turn to share, my stance would be centered largely around my Christian beliefs.

But that day, when we had our discussion, something unusual happened. Whenever I brought up anything related to my faith, it got shot down immediately. I was surprised; normally, my two Christian friends backed me, and I got at least an understanding nod from my other two friends. But that day, I got none of that. It was so strange. Somehow, unanimously, my friends decided not to listen to me anymore, and even went to the extent to tell me my Christian beliefs didn't count as an opinion.

That was the first time I had ever experienced opposition against my faith. Never before had my beliefs gotten in the way or caused any problems for me. And never in a million years had I thought my faith would cause problems with my best friends! I felt ostracized and couldn't figure out why my friends were acting this way.

A few weeks later, I found out why. During lunch, one girl in my friend group pulled me aside and told me one of our other friends was bisexual. Apparently, my bisexual friend had told everyone in the group about that, except me; she had feared how I would react because of my Christianity. I was surprised to find out she was fearful of my reaction, however, because her sexual orientation didn't matter to me. My faith wasn't that strong and she was one of my best friends! Nothing she was or wasn't could've ever changed that.

I was about to explain the misunderstanding to the friend telling me this news so we could just move on, but before I had the chance, she shut me up and blamed me for my faith. She blamed my Christianity for being why my bisexual friend couldn't be honest with the group and why our friend group could never be a completely safe and honest place. She made it sound like the simple fact I was Christian was negatively affecting the friend group.

I just sat there and took the painful punches of blame without expressing any emotion. I honestly didn't know how to react or what to say. I was taken aback, to say the least. I felt like an outsider and a reject. I felt alone and heartbroken, but I also felt wronged. It felt unfair that I was getting so many hits for a reaction my friends simply assumed I would have regarding my best friend's sexuality. And it felt unreasonable for that assumed reaction to be why my friends would suddenly make all these generalized conclusions about my faith affecting the group. Because of that, I tried to explain my point of view and how I never intended to affect the group in this way, but my friends had already made up their minds about Christianity.

From that moment onward, they only became more and more opposed to it. Our friendship spiraled downward by the day, and my friends' antagonism toward Christianity only got worse and worse. I could no longer bring it up or say anything about my faith without the fear of being ostracized. One day, everything climaxed to the point of my friends coming up to me and simply telling me to choose —them or God.

Impulsively, I blurted, "I choose God." Why did I say that? I honestly don't know. Maybe it was because I was done feeling excluded; maybe it was my fear of God if I chose my friends over Him. Maybe I wanted to see whether I would really lose my best friends simply because I believed in God. Maybe it was a combination of all those things. Whatever the true reason, it wasn't good enough or worth seeing my friends turning around and walking away from me for good.

I remember walking home that day, speechless and stunned at what happened. I mean, *I just lost my best friends*. After all those years of friendship, laughing together, crying together, and being there for each other, messing up but forgiving one another, and reconciling with each other—it was my Christianity that ultimately made me lose the only friends I ever had at school.

As I walked back home and reflected over everything that had happened, I got angry at myself. I was mad I had chosen God. Frankly, I was mad *at* God. The more I thought about it, the more I concluded that the only thing God had done in my life was make me lose my best friends.

And all for what? My half-faith that wasn't even that important to me?

As I was thinking all this, doubts and questions consumed my mind. During it all, the question my dad had asked me months before rang again in my head, but instead of hearing my dad's voice, I realized it was me asking myself, "Why was *I* Christian?"

I still didn't know. And that was what bothered me the most, especially now that I had just lost my best friends with no way of getting them back. I wanted to know why I believed in this Christianity thing I claimed to believe for the past fifteen years of my life. And I wanted to be confident in that belief. I realized, if my faith had been something I believed in with all my heart, it wouldn't have been as upsetting to lose or sacrifice things because of it. It was that I lost something so important to me because of a faith I was *unsure* about that made me straight-up angry. So, at that moment, I decided if I would lose friends over my faith, I better believe that faith with all my heart. I needed to know more. I needed to see if this God thing was truly worth the cost of losing my friends.

The search for God

For the next few weeks, I decided in my heart to try to get to know this God I had claimed to believe in my whole life. I was done just believing in Him simply because my parents did, or because I "felt" like I should. I wanted to believe in God for myself, so the first thing that made sense to do was read my Bible.

I looked at my small, pink Bible that had been collecting dust on my shelf for way too many years. I couldn't remember the last time I had read it. Hesitantly, I grabbed it and opened it to Genesis. And I read. Day and night, I immersed myself in this awe-inspiring, yet sometimes confusing, book. It was the first time I was reading the Bible as it was, not just watching some cartoon video about the stories at Sunday school. To tell you the truth, it was difficult to understand. Most of the time, the words just went straight through my head, and my efforts to read seemed fruitless.

But I was determined to learn everything I could about this God, so I kept at it. I was so determined that some days I stayed up half the night just to read. It's funny because I was never an incredibly determined person, but looking back, I think my determination came from a place of desperation. Feelings of loneliness and emptiness crept in as I felt the absence of my best friends in my everyday life.

Since I had never reached out or befriended any other people at school, I didn't have anyone to turn to during that time. The whole idea of God loving me and being there for me seemed more and more appealing. What fueled my determination to keep seeking Him was this place of genuine hope that everything the Bible said about God was true.

Days soon turned into weeks, and I eventually got to the New Testament and started the book of Matthew. As I was reading, I came upon a verse that made me stop in my tracks. I read it over and over and couldn't seem to take my eyes off it. It was Matthew

7:7–8: "Ask and it will be given to you; seek and you will find; knock and the door will be opened to you. For everyone who asks receives; the one who seeks finds; and to the one who knocks, the door will be opened."

It was as if my eyes were glued to this verse on my pink Bible's thin page. I couldn't look away from it. I was so intrigued by the confidence of this verse and how it didn't just say *some* of those who ask will receive; it said *everyone* who asks will receive. I became curious about exactly what I would find if I kept seeking this God, because from what I read in the Bible, it seemed like it would be good.

As I read the verse a few more times, I felt something inside me prompting me to pray, but just like with the Bible, I was hesitant; I couldn't remember the last time I had genuinely talked to God. I usually just said the same, repetitive prayers I was taught to say before meals and before bed, but something told me this was not the time to recite one of those "before meal" prayers. I felt a conviction to pray a real prayer. So, I got on my knees, closed my eyes, and prayed the most genuine words I had ever prayed. It wasn't super long or wordy, it was me just kneeling on the floor of my room and desperately telling God, "Honestly, I still don't know if You're real, and if You are real, I don't know if You are hearing me, but God, I'm seeking. I'm knocking. And this is me asking. You said in the Bible that everyone who seeks will find. When will I find what this verse is telling me I'll find?"

I constantly prayed like this for weeks, and to tell you the truth, nothing happened at first. I heard no audible voice. I felt no supernatural sensation, but I sensed the desire to want to know God more growing like crazy in my heart. The desperation was increasing as the loneliness and emptiness increased. So, I simply continued to talk to God genuinely, read the Bible constantly, and I desperately sought God. I kept circling Matthew 7:7–8 in prayer and hoped God would somehow understand what my heart was trying to tell Him.

In the following weeks, I also paid more attention in church. I was no longer just listening because I knew I had to answer my dad's questions, but because I really wanted to learn more about God. I was becoming interested in what my pastor was preaching about and genuinely wanted to believe in this God he kept saying was so amazing. Once I started listening better, this youth pastor soon became one of my favorite people ever. You just knew he cared so much; it was evident in everything he did and said. Because of his genuineness, I wanted to believe the God he always talked about was as great as he said He was.

I started to love going to church and hearing my youth pastor preach about God. I wouldn't say I honestly believed in Him yet, but I sure was on my way to believing. Everything was going so great. I finally felt like I was *now* getting to know who God really was. I was still seeking Him on my own and continuing to be fed by my pastor's words.

Amazingly, I was also growing in a deeper relationship with these two girls at youth group. Ever since I lost my school friends, these two girls filled that empty space my old friends weren't filling any longer. They would encourage me to keep seeking God, and before long, they became my two best friends—the only friends I had left.

For all those reasons, I walked into youth service every Sunday excited at what I would learn. Weeks went by, and I felt a little less alone and hopeless because I was constantly hearing the truth about God's love for me and being filled by the people around me. Our youth pastor did such an incredible job at making us want to believe in the God he believed in. Through his vulnerability, but boldness, in proclaiming the gospel, I wanted Jesus more and more every day. This pastor was someone I grew to love deeply and rely on as a leader and mentor.

A tough season

Because of that, I'll never forget walking into service one week and seeing my youth pastor crying. The room was silent as we watched our usually peppy and bright youth pastor in tears at the front of the classroom. It was clear something bad was up, but I never would have guessed it would be as bad as what happened. That day, he announced his resignation.

He was leaving. It all happened so abruptly that I didn't even have time to process what he had just said before the youth in the room were sniffling and wiping away tears, just like our pastor. Ever since we were little kids, this youth pastor had been like an older brother to all of us and he cared about each of the youth so deeply and personally. It wasn't long before the whole room was sobbing. Kids were crying left and right as we sat there heartbroken because of this sudden news. I was crushed.

With his departure, many kids in our youth group stopped coming to church regularly, and a handful of them even left the church entirely. It devastated our youth group to about ten kids from the twenty-five we once had. Thankfully, I still had my two best friends at church, but even that wasn't enough to stop the wave of hopelessness that came when it finally sank in that our youth pastor was gone. As weeks went by without being filled by God's Word, my desire to want to know God died down. My friends and I were all losing hope. I stopped praying and reading the Bible. I was no longer excited to go to church.

But crazily, that was only the beginning of the downward cycle that followed my youth pastor leaving. It wasn't long after I got close to those two girls at church that one girl ended up leaving because of all the discouragement. A few weeks later, we found out our senior pastor had quit unexpectedly, as well. It just so happened the one friend I had left at church was his daughter. Finding out our senior pastor was leaving was devastating because it also meant my last and only friend would be leaving with him. Because of the drama with his parting, I wasn't allowed to stay friends with her. I wasn't even able to say goodbye. She was just gone. Both my friends were gone.

But not only that, our congregation was falling apart right before our eyes. My dad, who was on the church's leadership team during that time, was trying desperately to find two new pastors to replace the ones we had just lost. Meanwhile, our associate pastor was trying his best to fill the role of the main pastor. Things were at rock bottom. Each week, we saw our attendance fall more and more. We didn't think things could get any worse.

But just like what always happens when people say things can't get worse, they did. Our associate pastor quit a few months later, which left us with absolutely no one. We had no youth pastor, main pastor, and now not even a backup pastor. I didn't even have the only two friends I had left. Our church's leadership tried for weeks to get replacements, but no one seemed to want the job. It reached the point where even my parents, who were church leaders, started losing hope. Our whole family did. My parents just wanted to leave, and as for me, I honestly wanted nothing more to do with God or the church.

My breaking point

Not only had God taken away my best friends at school, my favorite youth pastor, and pretty much my entire church, He had also just taken away the only two friends I had left. I told myself there was no way I could ever believe in a God who just takes away, so I stopped praying and seeking altogether. I was done with God and finished with church and with faith. I just couldn't believe it. Every time I either tried staying faithful to God or seeking Him, things just got worse. When I told my school friends I chose God, I lost them. When I wanted to know God, my youth pastor left. And when I found two amazing faith-filled friends, I lost them, as well. I didn't know what to do or even what to think. All I knew was that I desperately wished I had chosen my school friends over God that one day, because choosing God was not worth it. Not even close.

I wanted to run back to my school friends and tell them I was done with the whole God thing, ask them to accept me back, and say I'd never talk about God again. But my friends were long gone, and when I realized I could never restore the relationship I once had with my friends to the way it had been, I didn't know what to do anymore. I fell into a dark cycle of loneliness, emptiness, and bitterness. I closed myself off from people. I didn't want to talk to anyone, make new friends, or reach out to anybody.

So, I didn't. I told myself I didn't need people to be happy. I turned into this cold, unfriendly person. On the outside, I made it seem like I was perfectly fine, but the truth was, I was so broken and lonely on the inside that I would cry myself to sleep many nights and wonder if there was more to life than this. I constantly felt hopeless, worthless, and unbelievably empty, but I would never show it.

As I kept trying to maintain this fake outer image, I let all these negative emotions build up in my heart. I pushed them deep inside of me and kept them all to myself. It wasn't long before these emotions surfaced as pessimism, bitterness, and frustration.

I started to view all people and the world in general in such a negative light. I found no point, no purpose, and no passion for anything. Eventually, all this led to me isolating myself and hating being in the presence of others. I turned down people who wanted to hang out with me, refused to go to any social events, and lived my life feeling very alone.

I tried to fill this void in my soul with all sorts of things, the main thing being volleyball (which I'll talk about in the next chapter). I completely lost sight of who I was. I didn't know what to do or even where to search.

One night, I came to my breaking point. It was late and I was on the floor of my room weeping. I think everything just hit me that night. Memories I had suppressed of losing my school friends, my youth pastor, my church friends, and ultimately myself, consumed my mind. It was at that moment when some of the scariest thoughts I've ever had entered my mind: *Is it worth living? Should I keep living? Would anyone care if I stopped living?*

I was sobbing uncontrollably when, suddenly, God popped back into my mind as I remembered how, just a few months earlier, I had been so desperately seeking Him. I was so hopeless at this point that as a last resort,

I prayed. Even though I felt like God had been nothing but absent in my life, I remembered my youth pastor's words about God always being there for you and always being able to take you out of your loneliness. So, in desperation, I prayed on my knees. I was broken and alone, but that night, I felt a peace I had never felt before. As I was praying through my tears, I felt a quietness and stillness around me, and dare I say, I felt the presence of God ever so slightly.

You came from where?

I kept telling myself what I felt was not from God. I didn't want to believe it. It sounds strange, but it was more tempting to want to stay in the dark state I was in. It was almost as if I didn't want to feel hope. Maybe it was the fear of losing someone or something again if I gave God another chance. Who knows? I just knew I didn't want to want God. The next day, I overheard my parents talking about the whole church situation. They were discussing whether we should leave the church, so I stepped into the conversation to tell them we should just leave.

And let me tell you, we were so close to leaving, but during our transition period, our church suddenly got a call that someone wanted the youth pastor job. The call came out of nowhere, and the craziest part of it was, the girl who called was all the way from England! Her name was Esther and she was in Missouri finishing seminary school. She had no idea where she would go afterward until she found out about our church's job opportunity. When our leadership team asked her why she wanted the job, she replied, "I honestly don't know but I feel like God is calling me to Washington to take it."

When I heard the supposedly great news from my parents, I didn't really react. My heart had turned so bitter and cold since our old youth pastor's resignation that I couldn't be happy we found a new one. Everyone else was overjoyed, but to be honest, I was not happy. I was almost disappointed, because our family was so close to leaving and I wanted to be done with it. This new youth pastor was messing up that plan for me by making us stay.

The church accepted her right away, however, and she moved to Washington that month. A few weeks after she was hired, Esther came to guest speak for the youth. The only thing I recall from that day was that I was not open to liking her. In fact, I wanted her to be bad so I could tell my parents we should still leave. That's the mindset I had as I listened. I told myself no matter how good she was, I was not going to like her.

After she finished speaking, my parents excitedly asked me what I thought. Apparently, everyone loved her and couldn't wait for her to officially take the job. As for me, I told my parents the exact opposite of what they heard from everyone else. I told them I didn't like her. My parents were crushed. They were really hoping for a positive reaction from me because they wanted me to want to stay. My parents respected my decision, though, and for the next few weeks, they didn't let me stop going to church altogether, but at least they let me go to a different one. That was enough for me. I just wanted to be done with my old church.

After about three weeks of me going to this new church, my mom told me this Pastor Esther was holding a summer retreat camp. "What about it?" I asked my mom, to which she replied, "You should go, Izzy." I simply shrugged and pretended I didn't even hear her. There was no way I would go to that camp. I wanted nothing to do with those people, and I had no interest in whoever Pastor Esther was. But my mom was persistent. She told me she felt it would be great for me if I went. I kept telling her I wasn't going, but finally, she threatened me, saying if I didn't go to this camp, I had to go back to my old church. So grudgingly (very grudgingly), I told my mom I would go to camp—just so I could finally be done with that church.

As I picked up my packed duffel bag and boarded the church bus full of youth ministry kids, I looked outside the window to see my mom waving me off with a huge smile. She was so happy I was going. I, on the other hand, was not. I remember being so negative the whole ride to the campsite. On the bus, I sat by myself with my headphones in as the youth group cheerfully rode to the retreat center. I didn't want to be there. I had no hope and no expectations for the camp. I also had no interest in interacting with any of the youth, nor did I have any interest in listening to anything Pastor Esther had to say.

We arrived at the lodge and I mostly kept to myself. I didn't really talk to anybody and mainly stayed in my room. I made no effort to make friends with anybody and decided to see everyone in a super pessimistic lens. In fact, my pessimism got so bad that I got annoyed sometimes, just thinking about the youth at that camp with me. And naturally, the longer I was there, the more negative and closed-off I became, so it wasn't hard for people not to talk to me much.

Surrounded

Finally, it was Saturday night. I was relieved because we would go home the next morning. I sat in a chair in the back as Pastor Esther came to the front to give her last message. But instead of giving her planned message, she told us that she felt convicted by God not to share what she had prepared. *Um, okay then*, I thought. She said she felt like God was telling her there was some- one in the room who needed to just feel the presence of God. *Yeah, right,* I muttered. I laughed to myself at the craziness of Pastor Esther, boldly claiming God told her all these things, but she carried on and led us in a time of worship and prayer.

We all pushed our chairs to the side and gathered to stand in the middle of the room. Just a few minutes into the first song, Esther broke down crying as she poured her blessings and prayers over us. I just stood there awkwardly, watching as the youth around me joined Esther in singing. A few songs later, Esther led us in a song called *Surrounded*. It was a song I had never heard, so I tried to focus on the lyrics. The bridge went: *"It may look like I'm surrounded, but I'm surrounded by You."*

At first, I just stared at that line on the display screen in the front of the room, but as we sang that line over and over, I felt something deep in my heart. At once, I remembered all those days when, on the outside, it looked like so many people surrounded me, when in reality, I was so lonely. I recalled the moments when there would be so much love and friendship around me, but something inside still felt empty. Memories of the nights when I would cry myself to sleep and hopelessly stare up at my bedroom ceiling filled my mind, and I felt all those painful moments rushing back to me.

But it was in that moment of complete brokenness and pain that I felt something like a fire burning inside my soul. Suddenly, I felt a love I'd never felt before surrounding and supernaturally covering me. I felt an unexplainable peace and an inexplicable stillness.

Immediately, I fell to my knees. I took all my loneliness and emptiness to the floor with me and gave it all to God. It was then when I declared to God that I desperately needed Him and Him alone. Through my tears, I surrendered my life to Him and told Him I was so sorry for the way I had been living. I thought about how closed-off and unfriendly I had been, and how I probably hurt so many people because of that. But I just carried all that shame and guilt with me to the floor. Everything was falling off me—loneliness, emptiness, guilt, and shame.

While on my knees, as I lifted my hands to God, I felt His love completely cover me. Right then, I never felt more *surrounded*. All my life, I had felt so lonely and empty, but at that moment, I heard God's voice in my heart saying, "*You are not alone, Izzy, and you were never alone. I was always with you—on your hardest night and on your loneliest night—and all those nights were to lead to this night to show you how much you need Me.*" I knelt on the floor, stunned and speechless, because I knew I was feeling God's presence, and it felt amazing.

I felt free—free to be myself, to let go of all the weight I'd been carrying on my own, and free to be vulnerable and admit I was a sinner who needed Him. It was as if God was whispering into my heart that it was okay, and He still loved me despite the person I was, and He was still with me despite how lonely I felt. It was a combination of laying my life down before Him and Him overwhelming me with His supernatural love and presence.

I remember just weeping, because I realized God had heard my desperate prayers those months before when I was seeking Him. He showed me what I was looking for and trying to find, that missing piece, the filler of that empty void. That missing piece and filler of that empty void was *Him*!

He shattered my heart of the chains holding it shut. It was as if He were taking all the negativity, loneliness, and emptiness out of me and replacing it with love, forgiveness, and pure joy. I felt like light came down from the heavens into my broken and desperate heart, the heart that had closed itself off from people, the heart that had been filled with emptiness, the heart that had felt so hopeless and alone.

Right then, I realized all the loss I had experienced and all the loneliness and bitterness I had been feeling were for a reason. Those things were meant to push me to my breaking point so I would realize and understand how much I needed God in my life. That's why that encounter was so huge. It was because everything led to that moment, when I'd realize God was everything.

When I stood up again and opened my eyes, I knew for certain God had changed something within my heart. As I looked at the youth around me, I no longer saw them as people I wanted nothing to do with, but I felt this immense love for every single person in the room. It was as if God had opened my eyes to finally see clearly, to see the world as He made it. No better verse explains my transformation than Ezekiel 36:26: "I will give you a new heart and put a new spirit in you; I will remove from you your heart of stone and give you a heart of flesh."

That night changed my life. These people, whom I had once blocked out of my life and made no effort to get to know, now filled me with an overwhelming sense of love and compassion. I realized I *loved* these people, God loved these people, and that God had transformed my heart to love these people. God finally showed me what Matthew 7:7–8 promised. I had finally found it! God *showed* me His glorious light, *gave* me new life, and *opened* the door of my heart.

He took me, the broken teenager I was, and changed me through His transforming love and truth. He took my loneliness and replaced it with His powerful presence. He took my emptiness and replaced it with His radical fulfillment. He took my brokenness and replaced it with His life-giving restoration. And He took my coldness and replaced it with His supernatural love. That's what God does. God is love.

Wait, who are you?

I remember coming back from that retreat as a new person. When my parents asked me how it went, I simply told them I had met the Lord, and He had changed me. I remember them looking at me and asking if I was sure. I told them I was sure, but like most parents of a completely closed-off and unhappy teenager would react, they didn't believe me at first. I understood. I was aware it was a radical statement. Honestly, I was still coming to terms with the fact I *had* just experienced God—like *the* God.

But sure enough, as the days went by, my parents realized I had indeed met God, because everything in my life changed.

A bright light

The first change was with Pastor Esther. I decided to meet with her because I wanted to tell her how thankful I was for her and the retreat she put together. I also wanted to tell her that I was that person in the room who needed to feel the presence of God that Saturday night, and how, through the songs she led that worship session, I met God.

The more I think about it, the crazier it seems. I mean, how is it that God brought Esther to our church at the most perfect time? Then at the retreat I almost didn't attend, how had Esther felt God telling her someone needed to feel God's presence? And how is it that when she sang that song, God allowed me to feel His love and completely transformed my life on that night? That's crazy to me.

Anyway, we met and we talked for the first time. I couldn't believe I had ever thought I didn't like her and had closed myself off to such an amazing person. She had a brightness about her that just made me want to smile when I was with her. Every word she said carried so much grace and intentionality that I knew she genuinely cared for me. Her energy was so warm and inviting, that all I wanted to do was talk to her forever. As I kept smiling my way through our conversation, I tried to pinpoint what made her so bright. I had met many incredibly kind and caring people throughout my life, but never had anyone made me feel the way Pastor Esther did.

She made me feel loved and happy. *She made me feel God.* And that's when I finally pinpointed the difference: *Esther was different because she knew God.* She walked with God. She had a relationship with God. And because of that, she exuded God's loving presence to everyone around her. Her light shone radiantly through her.

No wonder everyone liked her that first day she came to speak for us! I just couldn't receive her at that time because my heart was so hardened. It was only because God changed my heart that I could see her for who she truly was. I could show and receive love in a way I never had before.

That day, I came home full of the energy I received from talking with Esther. It was the first time I had experienced God through a person, and it was the first time I realized that finding God doesn't just change your life, but has the potential of changing someone else's life. I saw this through the impact Esther had on me that day.

I continued to meet with Pastor Esther regularly. She quickly became someone I looked up to greatly as a faith mentor and an amazing friend. She inspired me to want to know Jesus more and was the one who encouraged me to write this book. It's absolutely crazy to think I wanted nothing to do with her before, because if it hadn't been for her, I would not be at my church anymore, there would've been no retreat, and I wouldn't have met Christ. And, of course, without her, this book would never have been written. That's how amazing God is.

And so, it was a culmination of a bunch of different factors that ultimately led to that night at the retreat when the whole trajectory of my life changed. The rest of this book is about all these radical changes and the parts of me that I found through finding this amazing God. I hope, as you read through these next chapters, you also find God for yourself and you will be transformed by His overwhelming, reckless, and unconditional love.

2

Finding Identity

"How did you find your identity in Christ?"

Finding your identity is hard. I know because I struggled with this for so long. In a high school environment, everybody is known for certain things, whether it's being an athlete, super smart, or beautiful; everybody is trying to find "their thing." For me, that was volleyball.

Growing up as a bit of a tomboy, though, I never thought I would end up playing volleyball. I was always more into basketball and soccer. When I was in fifth grade and my mom told me I should try volleyball, I immediately told her no. *That's a girly sport*, I'd always say, but with a bit of convincing from my mom, I tried it. And let me just say, I fell in love with the sport the moment I started playing.

Volleyball became everything for me. I joined my first competitive club team when I turned twelve and was addicted ever since. During middle school, I would plaster my room with motivational volleyball quotes, decorate my binders with a bunch of volleyball stickers, and I mentioned the word volleyball in my Instagram bio at least ten times. Saying I loved volleyball would have been a massive understatement. I'd say I was obsessed.

As I got older, I got more and more serious about the sport. I remember working with so much determination during my eighth-grade year and that following summer, because I really wanted to make the varsity volleyball team in my freshman year of high school. I wanted to be that one freshman who made it. I thought that would impress people, and I desperately desired that affirmation from others. As I did a little research, however, I realized only a few freshmen had ever made varsity in the school's history, so I knew I needed to work that much harder.

And when I say I worked that much harder, I mean it. I gave it everything I had. Every day after school, I rushed home and went out to practice in my backyard. I used the outside wall to practice my serving, the basketball hoop we had in the back to practice setting to a target, and the rest of the space to run lines and condition myself. And then, every night before I went to bed, I would lie on my back and set the ball to myself until my arms hurt. I would practice during every spare moment, because I was committed to getting that spot on the varsity team.

Getting that varsity spot was my only focus that entire year. I didn't think about anything else, didn't hang out with any friends, nor do any other extracurricular activities. I kept telling myself, *you have to get that spot, Izzy. What will people think of you if you don't get that varsity spot? You're going to be a failure. This is all you've ever worked for. Everything is riding on this. This is who you are.* I pretty much put volleyball so high on a pedestal that, in my mind, there was no plan B. Volleyball had become my life. It became who I was. It became my *identity*.

Tryout day

The day of tryouts finally approached and I was so nervous. This was it. This was my moment. I vividly remember walking into the gym as a tiny little freshman among a sea of talented seniors, but to be honest, I felt prepared. I knew I had done everything I possibly could leading up to that moment. So, I went all out. I played as hard as I could.

About halfway through the tryouts, they split the group of about seventy people into three different courts. The first court was the best, the second was the next best, and the last court was in some obscure location at the bottom of the school, so it was obviously the worst court. I was put on the first court. And boy, I was so excited. I was with all the talented seniors and tall girls on the varsity team the year before, so I was confident I'd get picked.

The end of the tryouts came, and the coaches told us they would email the results sometime that evening. I remember just sitting in front of my computer, waiting for that email all night. My hands were sweating, and my heart was beating faster than ever, anticipating the results that were either going to affirm or crush me. Finally, it came through. I quickly told my mom to come over to my computer, and together we read the list for varsity. I probably looked up and down the list five times, but my name wasn't there. I didn't make it. I continued down the email and found my name at the top of the Junior varsity list. I had missed the varsity team by one spot.

I was devastated. I couldn't believe it. All my hard work and the time I had spent in dedication hadn't paid off. All the relationships I ruined to pursue the sport hadn't paid off. I broke into tears. I couldn't stop crying. I know it sounds dramatic, but I really felt like my life was over. I didn't even know who I was anymore.

I wanted that varsity spot so badly. I felt that landing on the varsity team would make people see me as the amazingly talented player I wanted them to see. I wanted to be better than the average freshman who made the JV or C team. I wanted to be the best because this was what I had given my life to; this was the only thing going for me. I felt if I wasn't the best at the only thing going for me, then I would be nothing.

Eventually, however, I told myself I just had to work harder. That year on JV, I continued to practice and practice to make the team the next year. Then a crazy thing happened. One girl on the varsity team who played my position got injured. She was out for the rest of the season. Immediately, the coach called, telling me I would be moved up. And let me tell you, I was ecstatic. Obviously, I was sad for the injured girl, because she was a great player, but all I could think about was myself and all the praise I would get. All I could think about was how people would view me, now that I was on the varsity team. Now that I was on varsity, I completely forgot those thoughts about "my life being over" and "not knowing who I was anymore." It was as if making the team had restored my identity. I was happy again.

My debut

But of course, the grass is not always greener on the other side. I was benched all the time when I was first moved up. There were two other setters (the position I played) before me in seniority. So, for the first few games, I sat watching my team play. This was so frustrating. I knew I should've been thankful I could even be on this team, but my pride and insecurity couldn't be satisfied just with that. I wanted to play; I wanted to get the recognition and glory.

So again, I worked and worked, and eventually, I got pretty good and it was clear in practice that I deserved some playing time. But because I knew I was still younger and more inexperienced, I didn't expect to play just yet, especially since the next game was for the championships. It was a super big deal, and my team was nervous because the team we were playing was very good.

As usual, I sat at the end of the bench and waited for the spokesperson to call out our starting six players. I always envied those starting six. Getting my name called for the beginning lineup had been my dream ever since I started working toward it in the eighth grade. In my eyes, it was the highest honor; it was when everyone applauded for you as you ran onto the court to take your position.

Anyway, I knew for sure I wouldn't be called this game, so I zoned out. Then suddenly, I heard someone call my name. At first, I thought I had misheard, so I just kept sitting, but when my coach ran down to where I was sitting and told me to hurry up and get on the court, I realized I had actually been called. I practically jumped out of my seat and ran onto the court. Although it felt amazing to hear people cheer for me, I was incredibly nervous and confused. I didn't understand why, out of all games, my coach put me in the championship match. Nevertheless, I quickly took some deep breaths and went back to the baseline to serve the first ball.

I played the entire game and led my team to victory. It was our school's first championship win in twenty years. All my hard work and dedication had paid off! The girl who didn't make the team was suddenly a starter who played all the way around and never came out. That was my first "debut" as the freshman on varsity, the title I had always wanted. I remember, after that game, both my parents came up to me and told me they had never been prouder of me. My coaches then told me I had done amazing, and they expected great things from me. Then my classmates who had been watching the game also came to congratulate me and praised me for doing so well.

I was bombarded with all these comments from people, and I will say, it felt good in the beginning. People were giving me the acknowledgment and recognition I desired. *That's what I had always wanted, right?*

But as I kept playing as the starting setter for the rest of the post-season, I felt the pressure of having to fulfill the expectations of my coaches and parents. Hearing everyone tell me all these great things went to my head, and I let those thoughts consume my mind to the point where I would constantly stress because I felt like I wasn't doing enough.

Things became really unhealthy when my happiness began to depend on whether I played well in a match, or my coaches told me I did a good job. I let volleyball define my self-worth and my value. When I played well, I would feel affirmed and content, but when I didn't play well or got negative feedback from my coaches, I would become frustrated, tell myself I wasn't good enough, and feel I was disappointing everyone. I would start to lose my confidence, happiness, and, most crucial of all, my identity. I would lose myself.

An unhealthy cycle

Volleyball became something I no longer enjoyed. Instead of loving the sport for what it was, I became obsessed with getting good and then being accepted to play at a great college, so I could make my coaches and parents proud. I did it more for the praise of others than out of genuine love for the game. What once started as a hobby quickly became something of great stress and worry for me. And because I didn't want to let anyone down, I told myself I had to keep going, keep playing, and keep improving. I just had to.

I entered a downward spiral in which I felt chained to volleyball and to the expectations people set for me. I felt chained to having to become this athlete everyone wanted me to become. There was no way out. Volleyball was it for me. That was who I was. If I didn't have volleyball, I would be nothing.

A new identity

That's what I had thought my whole life. I thought there was no way I could escape the chains of volleyball that made me feel I had to constantly prove myself and be the best. But that night, at the retreat, when I found God, *everything* changed. God broke those chains for me with His reckless love. I remember coming back from that retreat simply thinking about Jesus and how amazing it was I could live for Him, instead of living for all the other false idols in my life. To be honest, when I came back, volleyball was not even a thought in my mind. It was pretty crazy that what used to be everything to me suddenly became unimportant in the bigger picture I was now seeing.

I didn't want to live for volleyball anymore, and I realized I didn't have to because God showed me a way out. I no longer had to drown myself in all the pressures and expectations that came with volleyball, because I had nothing to prove to the most important person in the world! The Almighty God of the universe loved me. He wanted me and was proud of me. I mean, He made me fearfully and wonderfully in His image!

When I compared volleyball to God, I realized how small and trivial the sport was. I realized how pointless people's praises and comments were, compared to the overwhelming embrace I get to receive from the God of love. I realized how temporary the satisfaction from volleyball would be, compared to the everlastingly fulfillment I get to have with the Lord. And when I accepted these truths for myself, I wanted to live for God, Someone who didn't require me to try to play well to receive affirmation. God never made me feel like I wasn't good enough, or had to prove my talent and ability. He still loved me and was proud of me, no matter what I did or how well I played.

By allowing me to experience His unconditional love and grace, God showed me that my self-worth shouldn't have to depend on whether I'm one of the starting six players, or if I play well in a particular game. Why? Because my identity was in Him, not volleyball. He already chose to love me unconditionally just as I am. His love wasn't like the love I received from my coaches and friends.

His love was the kind of love that sent His Son to die for me. The God who knew everything about me, the best and the worst, chose to love and accept me no matter what I did. Realizing that was huge for me. I felt as if God completely lifted the pressure to do well in volleyball off my shoulders; there was nothing for me to prove anymore. God loved me, and His love didn't require anything from me.

The amazing thing is, *you* have nothing to prove either! Maybe there's something in your life right now that's filling you with a lot of pressure and stress. Or maybe you feel burdened or "chained" to something you feel you just can't get out of. Maybe it's your sport, instrument, grades, appearance, or popularity. Everyone has something. And don't get me wrong, it's great to spend time with and think about all these things. What's not so great is when these passions become unhealthy obsessions.

When we let these things take over our lives to the point where they consume us with all the pressure that comes with them, we place our identity and worth in those things. Do you have something in your life that would make you feel less worthy or confident if you didn't have it or it was taken away? Or maybe you have something in your life you depend on for your happiness and affirmation. I sure did. And if you do, too, I want to remind you of what God reminded me about when I struggled with the same thing.

From one teenager to another, I'm confidently telling you that God loves you and is proud of you, no matter how well you perform, how good your grades are, how pretty you look, or how popular you are. How freeing is that! These things that may seem so important to us don't matter one bit to God when it comes to how much He loves us. His love should be the only thing we seek because it's the only love that matters. His love is eternal and unconditional. His love is not based on your works or your achievements, but on who He is, a loving God. Because He is who He is, we get to be who we are—children of the King.

I love what 1 John 3:1 says about who we are: "See what great love the Father has lavished on us, that we should be called children of God! And that is what we are!" (NIV). Wow, I love that. You aren't your sport, your grades, your appearance, or your popularity. *You are a child of God.*

Think about it. Most of the ways we use to describe ourselves are our names, hobbies, and relationships. At least, that's how I used to describe myself. I defined who I was by my name (Izzy Koo), the things I associated with (being a volleyball player and a student), and sometimes my relationships (a daughter, sister, and friend). But I realized, even if all those things were taken from me, I'm still somebody. It's not like getting a new name, quitting playing volleyball, being a student, and losing all my relationships would somehow make me nobody. I would still be somebody.

And that's where we come to a seemingly difficult question that philosophers have debated for centuries and continue to debate today: What is something that, if taken away from you, would make you nobody? The answer to that question would be who you really are.

This is where I realized the only thing that could be taken from me that would make me nobody, would be if I didn't have God. If there was no God, there would be no me. Everything else you can think of—sports, hobbies, relationships, names—don't define who you are. They can be what you do, who you connect with, and how you choose to label yourself, but you can only find your identity and who you are in Christ. *You are a child of God.* That is who you are. That's how I can be confident my identity is in God, because it's the only thing that, if taken away from me, would make me nothing.

The big decision

If you're anything like me, you might be thinking, *Okay, I get that my identity is in Christ, but what does that look like exactly? Does it mean I have to quit my sport and the things I love to do? Does it mean I should solely be pursuing God? Is that what it means to make God the center of my life?* If you are wondering any of these things, know these questions are completely valid; they are the same questions I asked myself in the beginning.

At first, I considered giving up volleyball. I thought my favorite sport couldn't be anything but an idol to me, so quitting was the best thing I could do to solely pursue God as my identity. (Just a side note: this was a crazy thought I was having. Never in my wildest dreams would I have even imagined thinking of quitting. I had always equated giving up volleyball with giving up the only thing I had going for me). It was only through the assurance I knew I had in God that allowed me to know I could give up volleyball. I knew, even if I lost it, I would still be who God said I was. I would still be (and am!) His child and He would still love me unconditionally.

This thought occurred around the summertime, and volleyball tryouts for the next season were just around the corner. I knew I had to decide fast, but I wasn't sure what I wanted to do yet. My mind was telling me to just quit volleyball, but my heart told me to keep praying. So that's what I did.

A life-changing message

This decision had been on my mind the rest of the summer as I thought about whether I would play the next season. Around mid-summer, my family and I went on vacation to Korea. By the time of this vacation, however, tryouts for the upcoming season were near, so I continued to pray about what I should do. I remember praying long and hard about my decision one Saturday night while we were in Korea. I asked God to give me some kind of sign to confirm what He wanted for me. I asked Him for guidance to help me make the right choice.

The next morning, my family and I were planning on visiting this church that had gotten some fairly good reviews on the internet. I was excited to go because I loved visiting different churches—especially ones in different countries. But the next morning, when my parents woke up, they told me they wanted to just stay in the hotel and have service as a family instead. They said the drive was far anyway, and it would be too much of a hassle to get both my little sisters ready to go within the hour.

Usually, I would've just agreed. What my parents said made sense. My little sisters were always cranky in the morning, and to catch a taxi within the next hour would take a lot of work on everybody's part. Plus, home services with my family were always great, but for some reason, I felt something inside me telling me I *had* to go to church that day. I don't know how to explain it. I just *had* to go.

I attempted to convince my parents that we just *had* to go to church, but they were both pretty set on staying at the hotel. My sisters were also still sleeping, so that didn't help my case. So, I decided I had to take matters into my own hands. I quickly woke up both my sisters and helped them dress and get ready. I then had them stand by the door while I went to my parents to practically drag them out of bed. My parents got up, despite being tired, and after much convincing on my part, they finally agreed to go to church. My dad quickly called a taxi, and the five of us ran down from our room to catch it.

At last, we were all sitting in the taxi on our way to church. My sisters were half asleep, and my parents were groggy and stressed because we had almost missed our ride. As for me, I felt complete peace. Something in my heart was pulling me to this church. When we arrived, I got this oddly comforting feeling I was where I was supposed to be. I just knew it.

I practically skipped my way through the church doors while my family sleepily came in behind me. The five of us walked into the main service room and waited for the pastor to come out and speak. But to our surprise, it wasn't the senior pastor who came out, but the youth pastor. In the corner of my eye, I saw my dad groan because he was probably thinking he came all the way here to hear a youth pastor speak. The pastor looked to be in his late twenties, and he announced it was his last day working at that church after three years. That day, he was giving his final message. *What a coincidence for us to be here on his last day*, I thought.

After the youth pastor finished his introduction, he flipped the PowerPoint slide to the screen with the message title that he would speak about that day. And believe it or not, the title of his message was: *Uniting your two passions of faith and sports*.

I literally gasped in my seat. Even my parents turned to look at me with shocked faces, as they both knew I was seeking direction and guidance about the choice I had to make soon about volleyball. I had just prayed about my decision the night before, and here was this youth pastor talking about exactly what I had prayed so hard about. Crazy how God works, right? I mean, it still blows my mind that God set it up so we would be in that church in Korea the day of that youth pastor's departure, and his message would be the exact message God wanted me to hear. Wow. Anyway, I sat there stunned as I found myself resonating with every word this pastor was saying. I felt like he was speaking directly to me.

His message was about how, when he was younger, baseball had become his idol. Like what I had experienced with volleyball, this youth pastor had made baseball his identity. The sport took over his whole life, but when he met God and found his identity in Christ, he realized he wanted to live his life for God instead of baseball. However, he thought that in order to do so, he must give up baseball entirely. He didn't think it was possible to make God his identity while still holding on to his sport. And for that reason, he ended up quitting baseball and choosing God, which ultimately led him to become a pastor. But it was his last day working at that church because God had revealed to him something that completely changed his perspective on sports and God.

He felt God calling him to join the FCA (Fellowship of Christian Athletes). This organization believes in uniting your two passions of faith and sports. Basically, this youth pastor explained that identity in Christ doesn't mean giving up whatever you enjoyed doing before. It's doing what you enjoy doing, but having God at the center of it. For him, having God at the center allowed him to use what he formerly idolized to honor God. As part of the FCA, this youth pastor was going to use baseball as a platform to tell people about God, and to train younger players both physically and spiritually.

This pastor realized baseball wasn't his identity, but simply a gift God had given him to glorify Him. He realized baseball, in and of itself, was never bad, it only became wrong when he made it an idol over God. But when the pastor put God at the center of his sport, he was no longer playing baseball just for the sake of playing baseball—he was playing for God. He took the very thing he loved and was passionate about and turned it into a tool for the Kingdom.

If you saw that pastor on a field playing baseball one day, and asked him what he was doing, he would probably answer with something like, "I'm just out here glorifying the Lord." And it's because he wouldn't be defining himself by the sport he played, but rather by the constant and secure confidence he has in his identity in Christ.

I was amazed by this youth pastor, but more than that, I was amazed by God. First, because God had answered my prayer overnight, but second, because I realized I didn't have to choose, either. Just like the youth pastor, I realized I could play volleyball but have my identity rooted in Christ. I learned having your identity in Christ doesn't mean you have to give up whatever you enjoy doing. God can shine through anything and everything you do, if you choose to make Him the center of it.

My audience of one

When I went to my high school's volleyball tryouts a few days after we came back from Korea, I went in with a completely different mindset. I told myself I wasn't playing for volleyball anymore; I was playing for God. And, oh my goodness, that simple mindset switch changed everything for me. First, I was not nervous. I wasn't stressing out about how well I would do, or what the coaches would think of me this year, because I knew I was free of all those expectations. And I found the sport was so much more fun when I wasn't always thinking about whether I was playing well enough. Having all that stress and pressure removed from me allowed me to just enjoy the game for what it was.

Second, by putting God at the center of my sport, He helped me do more than just play. For example, He gave me the courage to reach out to the new freshmen trying out for the team and help those around me who were stressed and nervous. God opened my eyes to be more aware of the people He placed next to me, rather than being so caught up with myself. I was not only *not* playing for volleyball, but I also wasn't playing for me anymore. I wanted to play hard, encourage my teammates, and play fairly because I was playing for God— my audience of one. Volleyball was no longer my idol nor my identity, God was. And when God became the center, volleyball just became a gift, a gift I could use to glorify Him and love on the people He placed in my life.

That day, I learned there was a huge difference between playing a sport for the sport versus for God. When you play with the sport being your idol, you feel pressured and stressed to play well and impress people; you feel like your self-worth and affirmation are dependent upon your performance. The sport becomes the source of your mood, happiness, and well-being. And as I've learned, sports are a very unstable foundation for all those things.

However, when you play with God at the center, you no longer feel any pressure to prove yourself or meet someone's expectations; you know your performance does not define you. You know your value and worth do not come from how well you do or how much praise you get from others because you are confident in the truth that you are treasured by the most high King. When you realize you can be confident in who God says you are, you can play your sport, or whatever activity you do, freely and without trying to meet any kind of expectations. You can even use your sport or any gift God has given to you to glorify Him and spread His name. And the crazy thing is, all this can happen with a simple identity switch.

Spread of freedom

Before I close this chapter on identity, I want you to know that placing your identity in God doesn't just affect one aspect of your life. For me, this freedom I found through Him didn't just stop at volleyball, it spread to all other aspects of my life. Whether I had thought my grades, what other people said about me, or how I looked defined me, I realized that placing my identity in Christ meant nothing defines me but God. And God defines both you and me as His child—precious and loved beyond measure.

3

Finding Confidence

"How are you so confident?"

I was the opposite of confident growing up. Ever since I was little, I was very shy. I remember so many times when my family and I would be eating at a restaurant, and my mom would tell me to go ask the waiter for more napkins or something simple like that. And I kid you not, every single time my mom asked me to do something that required talking to a stranger, I would have a mini panic attack. I was so fearful that when my mom turned to look the other way, I would quickly whisper to my sister (who was only about eight or nine at the time) to go get the napkins, instead. My sister would then sigh, look at me

50

with disappointment, and proceed to do the task assigned to me, but with no fear or nervousness whatsoever.

And if you're reading this and thinking, *Well, that's when you were younger. Everyone is afraid of talking to strangers when they're little kids,* let me just tell you, this lasted longer than when I was just a "little kid." It lasted until I met God, which was the summer before my sophomore year. Yes, you heard me right. I was a full-on teenager asking my little sister to go talk to waiters and cashiers in my place, because I didn't have the confidence to do so myself.

Talking to strangers was a nightmare for me. Well, let's be real. Talking to pretty much anyone was a nightmare for me. I was always so nervous. I would constantly think, *Will they like me? Will they think I'm weird? How am I going to keep the conversation going? Will they get bored? Do they even want to hear what I have to say? Do I even have anything to say?* My mind would constantly be bombarded with doubt, insecurity, and, to put it simply—fear.

For that reason, I struggled so much with confidence my whole life. I was that quiet kid in the back of the classroom who never raised her hand or made any effort to get to know somebody. I couldn't make a conversation last longer than, "Hi," and that's assuming I got to even saying "Hi" in the first place.

When I started my freshman year of high school, I pretty much concluded that speaking and socializing with others was just not my thing. I decided I wasn't good at it, and that I would never be good at it. I just couldn't get over all my massive insecurities, and those insecurities weren't just in speaking and socializing. They also had to do with my intelligence, the way I looked, my ability to play volleyball, the way people viewed me, my braces, how my voice sounded, etc. I could go on and on about all the things I was insecure about, and I'm sure you can too.

But for me, my greatest insecurity was talking to other people. There were just so many unknowns. *They might ask me something I don't know the answer to. I might bore them by the way I talk. I might talk too long or too little. My voice might crack. I might say something wrong and they won't like me anymore.* You get the point.

Confidence doesn't come from you

However, what I realized was that I was looking for confidence within myself. And when I did that, I found nothing in me that was worth being confident in. All I saw was insecurity. All I saw was doubt. All I saw was fear. One of the biggest things that changed when I met God was where I looked for confidence. God showed me that if I chose to be confident in who He was and what He was capable of, anything was possible, because there is no insecurity, doubt, or fear in God. God is perfect.

And since God is so perfect, we have reason to be confident in Him. Not only that, but the Bible tells us we can *boast* in our weaknesses and insecurities *because* of the confidence we have in God's strength and power. God says in 2 Corinthians 12:9, "My grace is sufficient for you, for my power is made perfect in weakness." *His* power is made perfect in *our* weakness. That means we can be confident in God's ability, even when we doubt our own. When I started having confidence in God instead of limiting myself to my fears and incapability, I broke out of the shyness and insecurities that had held me back my entire life.

Going up to strangers

There was absolutely no way I could be shy about talking and socializing with people anymore, because God had shown be so many reasons why I could be confident in Him. God had transformed my life from the inside out. God had filled me with a spirit of love and power. God had ignited a passion within me, and when He did, it was as if all my shyness and fear were thrown out the door and replaced by this new confidence I found in God's power and truth.

It was like I was a new person. I wanted to go out and tell everybody about God. I wanted to testify to everyone around me. Not because I had suddenly gained this newfound confidence within myself, but because I put my confidence in God. I was confident *God* could transform the lives of my friends. I was confident *God* could save my peers and *His* love was powerful enough to overcome any battles people were facing. That's why I felt like I could go out boldly, even in the face of my former greatest weakness. And don't forget, we're talking about the girl who couldn't even go ask the waiter for napkins!

Everyone gets a cross!

As I thought about ways I could share the gospel, the first thing I felt God put on my heart was to use my gift of crafts. Ever since rainbow loom became popular in 2013, I was obsessed. If you don't know what rainbow loom is, it's basically looping tiny, colorful rubber bands to make all sorts of things like bracelets and mini-charms. Anyway, I made about two hundred little cross keychains out of the rubber bands (Yes, that took a while!) and I brought a bunch with me wherever I went, and handed them out to anyone I saw. Whether it was the local grocery store cashier or the waiter at a fancy restaurant, I gave everyone these crosses I made, telling them God loved them so much.

I still remember the first one I gave to a craft store cashier. I slowly walked over to the check-out line so I could have enough time to reach into my purse and get out a cross. And I'm not going to lie, I was nervous at first. This was way out of my comfort zone, and no one was even forcing me to do it. It was just me wanting to tell this man about God because of the confidence I had found in Him. I had confidence that *God* could change this man's life!

It was finally my turn to check out. I walked over to the man and after he finished scanning all my items, I took a deep breath and felt God covering me with His peace. It was as though He was telling me, *Izzy, you can do this. Don't think about your shyness or your fear. Trust in what you have seen in Me. You may not be capable, but I am.* I looked up at the man, gave him the little blue cross I had made, and told him God loved him so much. He reached out his hands to receive it and gave me such a big smile. He told me thank you and hung the cross around this key ring near his station.

I walked away that day so happily. I almost laughed, because this was something I would never have had the guts to do on my own before. It was only because of God that the same person who couldn't even say "hi" to her classmates was now going up to strangers of all ages and backgrounds to tell them about the love of Jesus.

I continued to give out these crosses to everyone I met. Some people received them happily, some people were surprised to receive them, and some people received them with tears. The different responses from people were so amazingly overwhelming, but I want to share about one man who had a particularly powerful reaction. It's one I'll remember forever.

It was this worker at a popular burger restaurant where my family and I went to eat lunch one day. As my dad told this man our order, I noticed the man looked so tired and almost sad. He talked to us in a monotone voice, and it didn't seem like he was that happy to be there.

After he finished taking our order, I reached into my purse and pulled out one of my little cross keychains, but to be honest, I was a little bit more intimidated with this man than I usually was with most other people. The man looked to be in his upper forties, and he had this giant beard and dark eyebrows. His appearance was quite stern and tough. I must've stalled a little bit because my family was already heading to their seats and the man was already looking past me to ask the next customers what they wanted. So, I quickly cleared my throat and called for his attention. I then gave him the cross and told him God loved him so much.

He looked at me with surprise, but he accepted it gratefully. After I gave it to him, I went and sat down with my parents. I didn't think much of it after that, but as we started eating, the man called me over and showed me how he had attached the keychain to his car keys. He had this big smile plastered all over his face, so I happily told him I was glad he liked it. I then went back to enjoying my food, when suddenly, I heard this loud, booming voice coming from that same man. I immediately looked up and saw the same man who had somberly taken our order coming out from behind the cash register, excitedly greeting the new customers who had just walked in. And I'm not talking about a simple "hi" or "welcome." This guy was waving his hands and practically jumping as he greeted these customers with such enthusiasm and excitement that the whole restaurant turned to look. Everyone watched as this forty-something bearded man went up to all these customers, shaking their hands and welcoming them.

He even went over to all his co-workers, hi-fiving them and telling them how great a job they were doing.

This same middle-aged man, who seemed so done with his job and tired from work, was now the happiest and most enthusiastic man I had ever seen. My family and I witnessed him transform right before our eyes, and all this happened because of a little ounce of confidence. And by no means was that confidence from myself. I was not confident in my ability to speak to him or in whether his reaction would be good or bad. What I was confident in, however, was that God was in control, and that *He* could transform and remind this man of love.

It took just that little mustard seed of faith from me for God to work magically in the life of that man, because if you think about it, what I did wasn't much. I just gave him a measly little cross and told him the three simple words, "God loves you." But that's the amazing thing about God. He doesn't need you to do something extravagant, special, or big. He just needs you to trust Him. And let me tell you, when you trust God with all your confidence, He shows up. Every time.

I want to encourage all of you guys who might be struggling with confidence to not limit yourselves to what you think you are capable of, or what you can or cannot do. Instead, place your confidence in God and trust that He can handle whatever situation or insecurity you're facing. Never did I think that speaking to others or going up to strangers would be something I could confidently do, but here I am, giving middle-aged men tiny rainbow loom crosses to remind them God loves them. And it's only because I trusted Him with my speaking and put my confidence in Him that God showed up. He transformed that man at the restaurant just like I knew He could.

If God can do something crazy like that with me, He can absolutely do something just as crazy with you. It's not a matter of trying to make it seem like you are someone God can use or trying to fix all these things about yourself, it's a matter of believing that God is enough to cover any faults you have. It's believing God alone is awesome enough that it doesn't matter what we're scared of, what we're insecure about, what we say, or even what we look like. Those things don't matter. Confidence in God matters.

Unlikely people

It was in that moment at the restaurant when I truly realized how God can use one's weakness for His glory. I mean, who was I for God to use? Who was I for God to work through? I was a shy, insecure, and socially awkward teenager! Going up to random people and telling them God loved them was a million miles outside my comfort zone. But that's the thing. God doesn't work in comfort zones. God doesn't do the expected, nor does He use expected people. He uses the most unqualified and seemingly least likely people, so that everyone will see His glory when He transforms them.

Through this experience, I learned to expect God to do the unexpected. I learned God can and will use my weaknesses. I learned to believe that when we are a new creation in Christ, our lives will no longer be limited by what we think we're capable of, but what God is capable of. As I mentioned before, I couldn't talk to that man because I had suddenly become super confident in *myself*. No, I was still the same person and still had my weaknesses and doubts. But I became confident because I placed my confidence in God and in His promise that He gave me a spirit not of fear but of love and power (2 Timothy 1:7). I placed my confidence in the truth that God is for me (Romans 8:31), He is with me, and that He strengthens me (Isaiah 41:10). I stopped relying on my own strength and capability and relied on the One who told me: "Have I not commanded you? Be strong and courageous. Do not be frightened, and do not be dismayed, for the Lord your God is with you wherever you go." (Joshua 1:9)

Ever since that day with the waiter, I have never been the same. I realized I have nothing to be insecure or fearful about because it's not all about me anymore. It's about the God who lives in me, the God who works through me. With this new confidence I found, not in myself but in God, I also began to speak up in class, sat at the front in school, and started to love talking to people.

When I think about how I placed my confidence in God, I can't help but remember the story of David and Goliath. Goliath this huge giant standing taller than about nine feet, and he was incredibly strong. Anyone who knew about Goliath knew trying to fight him meant suicide. No one dared to challenge him.

Until David. Now David, as you know, was just a shepherd boy and just a teenager! He didn't have any experience in fighting, nor did he have any powerful weapons. All he had was a slingshot and a stone. What made David so confident? It wasn't his stature or his experience, it was the confidence he had in *God*. David saw God as bigger than anything—even a nine-foot-tall Philistine. David didn't dwell on his weaknesses because He knew all about God's strength, and trusting in God's strength was what allowed David to face Goliath so confidently. David knew, before he even stepped out, that He would win because God was on his side. I love what David said when Goliath threatened to kill him:

"You come against me with sword and spear and javelin, but I come against you in the name of the Lord Almighty, the God of the armies of Israel, whom you have defied. This day the Lord will deliver you into my hands, and I'll strike you down and cut off your head. This very day I will give the carcasses of the Philistine army to the birds and the wild animals, and the whole world will know that there is a God in Israel. All those gathered here will know that it is not by sword or spear that the Lord saves; for the battle is the Lord's, and he will give all of you into our hands." (1 Samuel 17: 45-47)

Wow. Look at David's bold confidence in the *Lord*. David didn't once doubt he would win because he had placed all his trust and confidence in God. It didn't matter that David was physically weak or inexperienced. All that mattered was that God's strength was enough for him. And when David knocked out Goliath with a single stone from his slingshot, it demonstrated not David's self-confidence, but rather God's power and glory.

Imagine if David went out on his own strength. He would've been crushed like a little bug! He would've been demolished within seconds. David clearly was the weaker person here, but because David placed his confidence in God, he knew he had nothing to fear. David knew it wasn't he who was fighting—but God.

A big night

As the days kept passing, I grew more and more in love with talking to all kinds of different people. In fact, talking to people became one of my favorite things to do! If you meet me now, you will probably never guess I used to be shy and scared of social interaction—which I think of simply as a testament to how transforming God really is.

About a month after that day at the restaurant, I was at church listening to Pastor Esther give her message. After she finished, she announced she was going to hold a worship and testimony night for us. When she said that, all of us got super excited. We loved listening to other people's testimonies—especially from the older college students and adults at our church. Unfortunately, our excitement immediately died down when Pastor Esther told us she wanted two *youth* students to share their testimonies.

As soon as she made that announcement, everyone kind of looked away, trying their best not to make eye contact with Pastor Esther. You know what I'm talking about? It's like that moment in class when the teacher asks a question and you don't know the answer, so you pretend to be busy doing something else. It was one of those kinds of moments. No one wanted to share, which was expected. I mean, it's nerve-wracking to be vulnerable and brave in front of such a large audience. Naturally, I also looked away. I never volunteered for these kinds of things. Talking and socializing with people was one thing, but giving a speech in front of a bunch of people was on a completely different level. My mind automatically flashed back to all those times in middle school when I would have to give a presentation or talk in front of the class. Those were the scariest days ever. My hands would be shaking as I watched my other classmates present, because I knew I could be called right after them. Anyway, I didn't even consider volunteering for this testimony sharing thing. There was no way I could ever do that.

No one raised their hand, so Pastor Esther just said if anyone changes their mind to tell her. She said otherwise she was just going to have some adults share. *Phew*, I thought. I was glad the suspense was over with.

But I felt unsettled. Suddenly, I got another flashback—but this time it wasn't about my scared middle school days. This time, I felt like it was from God. It was a flashback of the moment when I first met God at the retreat. Feelings of the light and love I felt that day filled my head and I was reminded of the amazing transformation God performed in my life. I then thought about how much my life had changed since then, and how much more fulfilled I had become. When I thought about that, I looked around to all the other youth students in that room and I saw myself in them. I remembered what it was like to live in fear, loneliness, and faithlessness. I remembered what it was like to drown in my own insecurity. And suddenly, I felt God urging me to volunteer to share. I felt Him telling me someone needed to hear what I experienced, someone needed to know their life could also be radically changed through knowing God.

I ended up telling Pastor Esther I wanted to share, but I'd be lying if I said I wasn't incredibly nervous. I had never done anything like this before. And for the record, I was terrible at public speaking. The fact I had volunteered to speak at a public event, without anyone forcing or pressuring me, was crazy, to put it simply. When I told my parents, they were shocked. They couldn't believe it. And to be honest, I couldn't either.

Nevertheless, I spent a lot of time in prayer with God and knew this was something He wanted me to do, not just to overcome my fear, but also to share the ways God had changed my life. In those moments I spent with God, I felt Him reminding me it was not about me, nor what I was or wasn't good at. It was about Him and that He would be with me the whole way. It was about Him that would speak in and through me. It was about the God who changed my life so that I *could* speak and hope to encourage others.

When I thought about it like that, it almost seemed selfish of me not to share. How could I not volunteer to tell other people how amazing God was after what He had done in my life? How could I not volunteer to give my testimony when there were young people who desperately needed to hear a message of hope?

For the next few days, I prayed and wrote and prayed and wrote. Eventually, the day of the testimony night came and, once again, the nerves crept in. As the night began and the praise team led the church in worship, I couldn't stop trembling. I couldn't focus on the worship because I was praying the whole time that God would give me peace and comfort. Finally, the worship ended and everyone took their seats. I sat nervously in anticipation as the tech guys fixed the microphone at the front. I knew I would be called up at any moment, and that moment came as soon as I thought it.

The amazing thing was, the moment Pastor Esther called me to the front, I felt complete peace. I felt God's presence with me. My mom, who was sitting next to me, asked me how I was feeling and I remember telling her my nervousness had left me. I was ready. I walked to the podium and picked up the microphone

As I looked around at everyone in the audience, I first saw my mom, who looked like she was going to cry because she was already so proud of me. Then I saw my dad, and honestly, my dad just looked confused because I don't think he had quite processed that his shy little daughter would actually be speaking. Then I looked at all my friends, looking at me with anticipation of what I would say. My friends there hadn't seen me since God had changed me, so I'm sure it was a shock for them to see me up front, as well.

I took a deep breath, put all my trust in God, and started speaking, and for the next fifteen minutes, I spoke with a boldness and confidence I never knew I was capable of. I spoke with a passion that could have only been ignited by God. The whole time, I spoke knowing God was with me and speaking through me— because I definitely could not have spoken like that on my own.

After I finished, I couldn't believe what had just happened. Here was the same person who would get C's on any kind of oral presentation, standing before her church and voluntarily giving a fifteen-minute speech. I'll remember that night forever. And the best part wasn't that I had spoken, but that God had spoken. I received so many encouraging texts from friends and parents who told me they were inspired by my story. Even people I didn't know came up to me, telling me they were encouraged to grow in their relationship with God.

That day was a huge milestone for me. Although I had learned to put my confidence in God before (through giving out the crosses and stuff), sharing my testimony that night took another huge leap of faith. But through that leap of faith, I realized God can truly do *anything*.

However, we can only see all that God can do when we first step out in faith. Think about it. My whole life, when I was still drowning in my insecurity, fear, and shyness, I never saw God do crazy things because I wasn't giving Him any opportunities to do them! I mean, why would God use me or work through me if I was closing myself off to the very possibility of Him using and working through me? It was only when I took those leaps of faith, by going up to people with the gospel or stepping up to give my testimony, that I saw God's incredible power in my life. In those moments, right before I took those leaps, God filled me with so much peace and comfort.

For example, with the testimony sharing, I was so nervous until right before I had to speak. I believe that was because God knew I was stepping out in confidence for *His* name's sake and for *His* glory to be made known. And God honors that. God honors when we step out in courage, in faith, and in boldness. Those are the moments He shows up and we get to witness the awesome power of Jesus.

That's why I firmly believe we do not have to live in fear or ever underestimate ourselves and our talents. God doesn't need us to do anything but trust Him. His ways are greater than our ways. His thoughts are higher than our thoughts. Let's rest in that truth. We are no longer limited to ourselves or our imaginations, we are limited to God's amazing transforming power—and that's unlimited.

A new creation

One of my favorite verses is from 2 Corinthians 5:17: "Therefore, if anyone is in Christ, he is a new creation. The old has passed away; behold, the new had come." This verse could not be truer. I know I mostly talked about how God helped me with my fear and insecurity of speaking, but I want you to know that once you choose to accept Christ and place your confidence in Him, your *whole life* will be made new. Imagine walking down the hallways of your school without being nervous about what you look like or what other people think of you. Imagine raising your hand in class without being afraid that you'll say something wrong or embarrass yourself. Imagine not letting any hurtful comments make you think less of yourself, because you are so confident in who God says you are. Imagine living a life of spontaneity, a life outside the box, a life that you *want* to live because it's just so exciting.

I'm telling you right now, you can have that life! There is a way to live without letting fear and insecurity stop you from becoming who God wants you to be and living the way God wants you to live. There is a way to walk in confidence wherever you go. I have found this amazing life, and I want you to know that all it takes for *you* to find that life, is to stop looking inside yourself for confidence and start looking toward God.

Place your confidence in God, trust Him, and go out of your comfort zone to do things for His glory. Put your trust in the God who is able. Put your trust in the God who has a plan for you. Put your trust in the God who helped small, little David beat the giant Goliath with a single stone, because that same God who was with David, is with you right now.

4

Finding Patience

"How do you have so much patience?"

I used to think patience was simply having to respond to someone or something without getting angry and yelling. I used to think patience was just holding back your true feelings and emotions and putting on a smile. But through my long, difficult journey of finding patience, I realized it's so much more than just your actions or facial expressions—it's all about your perception.

Olivia's perception
I have two younger sisters. The older of them is Olivia and she's currently eleven. Growing up, I've always had

a good relationship with Olivia, mainly because she was such a good sister to me. It didn't matter how mean or bad a sister I was; I could yell, scream, blame and lash out at her, but she would never hold any bitterness or anger against me. There have been countless times when I got frustrated or irritated with her for no reason, but instead of getting mad at me for being unfair, she would do everything she could to try to make me happy. Whether it was leaving me a thoughtful note or my favorite snack on my desk, asking me if I needed anything, to apologizing when it wasn't even her fault, she always had my best interest at heart.

I remember coming home from school almost every day in a really bad mood (pretty typical of how I used to be). I would be frustrated and irritated at who knows what, and I always took it out on my sister. When Olivia would come downstairs to say hi to me, I wouldn't even bother looking up to acknowledge her. Not only that, but I'd somehow blame her for putting me in a worse mood just by talking to me. But here's the thing about Olivia, she's not like any typical eleven-year-old younger sister. She doesn't ever retort by saying something like, "Hey! I just said hi to you, aren't you going to respond?" or "Why are you being so rude again?" No, she comes and sits right next to me to ask if I'm okay. She asks how my day at school was. But, of course, my impatient self would just get more annoyed at her niceness and I would tell her to leave me alone. And again, instead of getting angry, Olivia would just get up and leave peacefully. She knew I needed space and never made me feel guilty for yelling at her. But it's not only that, Olivia always goes one step further. After I'd finish my homework (or whatever I was working on that supposedly prevented me from saying hi back to my sister), I'd go to my room and almost always be greeted by something for me on top of my bed. Most of the time, it would be a card from Olivia. And inside the card, there'd usually be some kind of candy she'd won from school (which she saved for me instead of eating herself), as well as a note she wrote, saying she loves me and hopes I'm feeling better. I mean, how good a sister did I get? Honestly, if she wasn't so amazing, our relationship would've gone down the drain a long time ago. It was her over-abundance of patience toward me that gave our relationship a chance.

Sometimes, I would get so confused by her continuous acts of kindness and patience that I would literally sit her down and ask her why she was being so nice to me. I just couldn't understand why she would go out of her way to care for me and listen to me, when I was such a terrible sister to her. I didn't understand how she could be so patient with me when I was always so frustrating to be around. It was something I simply could not understand.

It was only later that I finally understood the reason. It was because of the way she chose to see me. I was her big, older sister, so no matter what I did or how terribly I treated her, Olivia still saw me simply with the eyes of a little girl wanting to be like her big sister. She was patient with my unfairness, bursts of anger, and uncalled for irritation, because those traits weren't the ones she chose to see in me. She chose to see me as someone she looked up to, someone she wanted to be like, and someone she loved. That was her perception of me.

My perception

I, on the other hand, did not have the same perception of my sisters that they had of me. This was especially true with my youngest sister, Noelle. She is currently seven years old, which means there is about a nine-year age gap between us. That's quite a lot of years, so naturally, I never had a close relationship with Noelle.

When Noelle was born, I felt like my life was turned upside down. Suddenly, my mom wasn't available to hang out with me like she used to, my free time started disappearing because I always had to babysit my sister, and all vacations were put on hold because Noelle wasn't old enough. It just seemed like there were so many things taken away from me because of her. I could no longer watch any movies with a rating higher than PG, I couldn't make any noise past seven, because that would wake up Noelle. I couldn't do this, I couldn't do that—it was like I couldn't do anything.

It wasn't long before I saw Noelle more as a burden than as my sister. She became an annoyance to me. I saw her as an obstacle in the way of my fun and freedom. And because I only saw her in that way, I was not very patient with her. Actually, "not very patient" is a dramatic understatement. I absolutely could not stand her. Every little thing she did annoyed me, whether it was her accidentally bumping into me, or her asking me to play, it usually ended up with me getting irritated and yelling at her.

It didn't matter how many times my parents told me to just give her a chance. It didn't matter that she was now getting older and forming her own personality. It didn't matter that I knew I was on the track to ruining our relationship forever. To me, she was simply an annoyance. That's how I chose to see her.

That label I put on her led to some mean and unfair actions on my part. I can recall several times when I yelled at her for no reason, was bitter toward her on purpose, or out of my own frustration, told her insensitive things I probably shouldn't have said. For the longest time, I thought my lack of patience toward her was just a character flaw. I thought I was just easily prone to getting irritable.

What I have learned over the years, however, is that my temper and impatience were never the issue. It was my mindset. It was *my perception*. Think about it. How are you supposed to show patience to someone you simply think of as an annoyance? How are you supposed to be kind to someone you've already decided is a burden to you? How are you supposed to love someone you look at as an obstacle to your freedom? The answers to all those questions are simple: *You can't*.

The Power of Perception

That was the first thing God revealed to me during my journey of patience; you can't show patience to someone unless you change your perception of them. For my whole life, I perceived my sister in a way that prevented me from showing love and patience toward her—as a burden, an annoyance, and an obstacle. So, whenever she tried to talk to me, of course I snapped back, was bitter, and lashed out. *She was just an annoyance, right?*

This clouded perception blinded me from seeing her for who she truly was and what her intentions were when she wanted to talk to me. Instead of perceiving a tap on the shoulder from Noelle as a sign she just wanted me to notice her or play with her, I automatically jumped to the conclusion that she just wanted to annoy me. Instead of seeing her trying to copy my outfits every day as a sign of her liking how I dressed and wanting to be more like her older sister, I assumed it was because she wanted to see me frustrated and irritated with her copying me. And instead of looking at her asking me to play as a sign she wanted to spend more time with me, I simply concluded she was just trying to distract me from whatever I was doing.

This distorted perception I had of pretty much anything my sister did caused my reaction toward her to *always* go first to anger and bitterness. It caused my responses to *always* be filled with impatience and irritation. That's the power that perception has. If it's negative, it will twist and manipulate even the most innocent and honest of intentions. It will cause you to believe there can be no good to come out of a person, because your mind only see's the bad in them. In my case, it caused me to never even give my sister a chance.

God's perception

It took God bringing me to my knees at that retreat, and removing my stone heart and the cloud blocking my eyes, for me to realize my perception was distorted. God opened my eyes to see the world as He saw it. And do you know what God's perception of us was when He first created us? *Very good.* God looked at us and said we were *good.* He didn't make us, see all the sin we committed and then decide we were burdensome or annoying. No, He did the opposite. When He made us, the first thing God did was form His perception of us. He saw us as good and precious. So even when we do commit sin or test God's patience, He shows us love and mercy—because to Him, we are His perfect and beautiful creation.

One of my favorite Bible verses is from 1 Peter 2:9. In this verse, God describes us as "…a chosen people, a royal priesthood, a holy nation, God's special possession…" I mean, how crazy is that? The God of the universe thinks of *us* as a royal priesthood. A holy nation. A people for *His* own possession. That's how special and valuable and loved we are in His eyes. That's why God shows us mercy. That's why God shows us love. That's why He shows us patience, because to Him, we are beautiful and precious beyond measure.

When I think about the way God looks at us, it always reminds me of how Olivia looks at me. She decided, long ago, that I was someone she would look up to, and I would be someone she wanted to be like. Most important, she decided I would be someone she loved. It didn't matter if I was unfair sometimes, if I got angry, or if I acted out in frustration in moments. Olivia was *patient* with me because of the *perception* she had of me.

When I first realized the power of perception, it was eye-opening. It was astonishing to believe God thought of me in that way. What was more eye-opening was that God also saw Noelle and Olivia in the same way. I realized, when God looks down from Heaven and sees my sisters, He sees His *beautiful creations*. He sees the two little girls He formed and crafted in *His image*. He sees the girls He *set apart* for His glory and His kingdom. For me to look at those same girls as annoying or burdensome? That's just an insult to God's creation.

This is just one example of the power a negative perception can have, but if you think about it, our perception plays such a big role in our patience level toward anyone and even anything. Think back to the last time you were impatient with someone. What was your mindset when you were talking with that person? Did you see them in a positive light going into the conversation? Did you give that person or thing a chance? I think, a lot of times, we go into life and our relationships with certain labels and judgments of people. And often, the way we see people influences the way we interact with them. With people we think of as burdensome and annoying, we find we are short-tempered, quickly angered, and easily irritated, even if those people haven't really done anything that should cause us to feel frustrated.

But what if we viewed everyone the way God views us? What if the next time we see that person we think is burdensome, we choose in our hearts to look at that person as God's beautiful creation? What if we get rid of our negative perceptions of people and replace them with the lens that God looks through? I think you will be surprised to see the amount of patience you will naturally exude when you see the person in front of you as precious, worthy, and beautiful.

Just as it's hard to be patient with someone we have already labeled as burdensome or annoying, I'd say it's harder to not be patient with someone we have chosen to see the way God sees them. I realized, once I saw people through the lens of God, the way I interacted with people changed completely. The people I once saw as frustrating suddenly became people I saw as created in the image of God. The people I once saw as my enemies suddenly became people I saw as God's beautiful creations. The random people I just met on the street became people I saw as so precious and loved by God. And it was only when I saw through this new lens that I realized it's the only lens we should ever look through. We don't just need a new perception, we need *God's perception*.

This Godly perception of Noelle is what began the healthy and flourishing relationship we have today. When I saw her how God saw her, I stopped seeing my sister as annoying or burdensome. Instead, I saw her as she was created—beautiful and full of light. She became one of my best friends.

A humbling experience

One of the biggest changes that happened in our relationship was that Noelle started asking me to see her to sleep. As a seven-year-old, Noelle still needs someone to tuck her in and read her a story before she goes to bed. That job was usually my parents' because I never had the patience to do it. I tried it once before, and all I remember is that when she asked me to read her a third story, I walked out of the room. Since then, Noelle has never asked me to see her to sleep again. But because she saw my change in attitude toward her, through me showing her so much more patience and kindness, I noticed Noelle wanting to spend more and more time with me. She now wanted to be with me, and eventually we got to the point where she wanted me to see her to sleep. I know it doesn't sound like that big of a deal, but it was pretty big. It feels oddly affirming to know your little sister wants you to see her to sleep when she could be seen to sleep by Mom. Anyway, I excitedly went to see my sister to sleep that night. We read books together and she kept telling me that I was being so much nicer. When she asked me why I had changed, I told her it was because I met God. I remember her just sitting there, thinking about what I had just said, but not saying anything. After a few minutes of silence, I told her goodnight and was about to leave, when suddenly, she blurted out a question. She asked me, "Can you tell me about God?"

I was caught off guard. My old self would've probably given some half-hearted answer and continued to walk out the door. But because my new self was blown away by this question that my seven-year-old sister just asked me, I stopped in my tracks. I slowly walked back toward her bed and lay down next to her. I quickly gathered my thoughts and told her all about God and how He loves her so much. She then asked, "How did you meet God?" Again, blown away by her genuine interest in wanting to know, I described the amazing feeling I got when I first felt God's love.

I explained that supernatural moment during retreat when I felt God removing my heart of stone and giving me a new heart to love and new eyes to see. I told her about the peace and the joy I feel every day now, and how just knowing God is with me gives me strength. I also added how God helped me change my perception of people and the world, so that I could show more patience and kindness. I think I got so lost in my own world as I was going on and on about Jesus, that I forgot I was talking to a seven-year-old. Once I returned to reality, I turned to look at Noelle, fully expecting to see her fast asleep or bored out of her mind, but when

I turned, I saw her eyes fixed on me and her face glowing with curiosity. She told me to keep going. So, I did. As I went on and on, I felt her tiny little body coming closer to me as she reached out to hold my hand.

She then looked up and asked me, "How can I meet God like you?" I smiled at her and told her she should read the Bible and pray if she really wanted to meet God. Immediately, she jumped out of her bed and ran to get her *Kid's Adventure Bible*. She brought it over and asked me to read it to her. And let me just tell you, I was overjoyed and amazed by my sister's desire to want to know Jesus, and the fact God had opened this window of opportunity for me to read and explain the gospel to her (literally at midnight). To be quite honest, I had never seen Noelle more passionate about anything. She never liked reading books, so her excitement to read probably the biggest book ever, was quite surprising. Her eyes were glued to the pages and she just wanted to keep reading more and more.

After we read for about thirty minutes, it was well past her bedtime, so I told her she should probably sleep, but she stopped me one more time to ask me one more question. She asked, "Can you show me how to pray?" So, I happily came back to her and we both got on our knees. I grabbed both her hands and I prayed for her. It truly was like feeling God's love from the first time I met Him all over again. I could sense the Holy Spirit in the room as I poured out my prayers and blessings over Noelle. It was a moment I'll never forget.

After I finished, she got under her covers, looked up at me and told me, "I feel so happy." She then told me I could go, but said she wanted to read more of the Bible with me tomorrow. Now, here's the crazy part. Noelle *never* lets me go. She often has nightmares, and most days, she wakes up saying she had a terrible dream. She also has a constant fear that something is in the room, so my mom or whoever is putting her to bed usually has to stay with her for the whole night. But that night, Noelle told me she had never felt happier. And she *let me go*. I even asked her out of shock, "I can go, Noelle?" And she said yes, but not only did she say yes, she said it was because she wasn't scared anymore. When I asked her why she wasn't scared, she said, "Because you said God is with me. I don't have to be scared anymore."

As I stood there, teary eyed and all, I replied, "You're right, Noelle, I did say that. God is always with you." And with that, I left and never felt so humbled in my life. That day marked the start of a whole new kind of relationship with Noelle.

Now, it may seem like that story had nothing to do with patience but it actually had everything to do with it. Let me tell you what I mean.

Noelle and I had never once had a conversation as long or as deep as that. Usually, when Noelle tried to talk to me or ask me a question, I would just cut her off or tell her to ask someone else. I simply never had the patience or the "time" to sit with her and just talk. Even when I did have time and would talk to her, I would quickly get ticked off if she asked too many questions or if the conversation became too long. It was because I never viewed it as a conversation with my sister; I viewed it as an obligation, something I had to do to minimize the crying in the house.

That's why that night with Noelle had everything to do with my patience. That kind of conversation and moment with Noelle could've never happened with my old self. Absolutely no way. Not only would I have never seen her to sleep in the first place, but I would've walked out the door after just saying goodnight, even if I was putting her to bed. But that night, I was not perceiving her questions as something obligatory that I felt forced to answer, nor was I perceiving that time as a chore with which I was tasked. No, I was seeing her questions as an opportunity for me to get to talk with my little sister. I was seeing that time as an opportunity for me to get closer with her. And lastly, I saw her as someone I wanted to be with, someone I wanted to love. The patience just came as a side effect of changing all these perceptions.

When you read about that night I just wrote about, I realize most people might see it as simply me getting to witness to my sister or us having a special moment together. But when I think about that night, I see it as the moment I realized the power of patience. And I realized it was the power of patience that allowed me to witness to my sister and have that special moment together in the first place.

But most important, the patience God gave me was the reason my relationship with my sister was restored. We now read the Bible and pray almost every night before bed. We now have long and deep conversations all the time. We now love being in each other's company. And now she has a genuine heart to get to know the Lord. All because of a little patience.

Patient, not perfect

With everything said, however, it doesn't mean I never get impatient with Noelle. And it sure doesn't mean she never annoys me anymore. She is only seven, after all. It just means I can respond with more love, understanding, and patience because I choose to see her as beautiful instead of as a burden. Still, there have been times when seeing her in that way has been hard. We are only human after all; we can't be perfect. Luckily, God knew we would struggle and provided us with the most important tool to help us—Scripture.

The importance of memorizing Scripture

I know most of you are probably groaning right now at the title of this section. I probably would be, too, if someone had told me to do this a few years ago. I had never really been into memorizing Scripture, because frankly, I didn't think it would be that helpful. I thought it was pointless, and I didn't understand why all my youth leaders and pastors were so obsessed with having us memorize a bunch of verses. But let me tell you, memorizing Scripture and engraining God's Word into my mind has been one of the most life-changing things I have ever done.

It all started when my good friend Nathan challenged me and our other friend Solomon to memorize a verse every day. We would all memorize one verse and then FaceTime at night to recite our verses to each other. To be honest, it felt like a chore at first. I would always forget to memorize my verse until right before we called, so I would anxiously cram a quick one in my head last minute.

But one day, I remembered the challenge early (I was pretty proud) and decided to memorize a couple of verses. The verses I chose were from 1 Corinthians 13:4–7: "Love is patient and kind; love does not envy or boast; it is not arrogant or rude. It does not insist on its own way; it is not irritable or resentful; it does not rejoice at wrongdoing but rejoices with the truth. Love bears all things, believes all things, hopes all things, endures all things."

After memorizing these verses, I went about my day as usual, but then a crazy thing happened. I was busy with homework when Noelle came up to me and asked for help on a project she had to do for school. This usually would've made me very irritable, and I probably would've told her to wait or to ask someone else. But suddenly, I heard 1 Corinthians 13:4–7 speaking to me, particularly the part about love being patient and not irritable. I almost jumped out of my seat because I felt like I was hearing God's voice. In that moment, a sense of patience came over me, and I went to help my sister with her project, with no grumbling or hesitation whatsoever. After I finished helping her, I was shocked at the amount of patience I showed. I couldn't believe it, to be honest. And the crazier thing was, as I kept going about my day, situations that would test my patience kept popping up and different verses I had memorized spoke to me. When my mom was about to do the dishes after dinner, Romans 12:10 popped in my mind and reminded me to outdo one another in showing honor. Almost automatically, I got up and told my mom I would take care of the dishes that night. And then, as I felt myself getting burned out by "outdoing" myself, Galatians 6:9 popped into my head and told me not to grow weary of doing good and never give up.

In Romans 7, it says if there was no law, we would not know our sin. I came to the realization of what that meant through memorizing Scripture. By memorizing verses, I started to know God's law like the back of my hand. And when that happened, I was becoming aware when I was about to do something that was not pleasing in God's sight, such as getting impatient or selfish. And by realizing that more and more, I could live my life better and show more patience and kindness to everyone around me. The lies that filled my head were suddenly replaced by the truth from the Word of God itself! And when you fill yourself with the Word of God and wear it like armor, the devil will have a difficult time trying to steer you off course.

That's why I encourage anybody reading this to start memorizing some Scripture! I know it might sound like a chore, or something pointless, but let me tell you, it is *life-changing*. Once you start equipping yourself with the Word of God, you are going into the battle of life armed with God's Word written all over your heart. The verses you memorize will be like swords you carry into war. Each piece of Scripture will fight against a certain lie that will try to grab hold of you. For me, 1 Corinthians 13:4–7 was my sword and I continue to carry that sword with me to help me fight my battle with patience!

5

Finding Purpose

"What is your purpose in life now that you know Christ?"

When I was a kindergartener, I thought my purpose was to grow up and become a famous artist. In elementary school, I thought it was to become a famous singer. That lasted until middle school rolled around, and suddenly, my new purpose in life was to qualify for the Olympics in volleyball. That one lasted the longest, but my point is, what I thought my "purpose" was in life kept changing as the years went by. One day I was set on doing one thing, and the next, I focused on something else entirely.

At the time, I thought it was just my purpose changing, but as I look back at all the times I jumped back and forth between all my hobbies, I realized maybe my purpose never changed at all. You see, the definition of "purpose" is: "the reason for which something is done," or "one's intention." And the more I think about it, the reason I ever pursued any of the things I did was to get approval and affirmation from other people. That was my true intention. That was the real driving force behind everything I did. It wasn't because I wanted to be the best artist, singer, or volleyball player just for my own satisfaction and happiness, it was because I wanted so badly to be recognized, known, and affirmed. I just used all these things to try to achieve the real purpose and motivation in my heart.

My whole life, I was ruled by this desire to get praise, approval, and affirmation *for myself*. It was always about *me* and what I wanted for *my life*. It was always about what *I* would receive from other people by becoming successful in the areas I committed to; it was always about *my* fulfillment and *my* happiness.

Honestly, I didn't think it was possible to get rid of that true purpose deep in my heart because, frankly, at the time, there was nothing more important to me than, *well, me*. But accepting Christ into my life changed that purpose for two reasons: First, when I met God, the desire in my heart that longed for people's approval was completely fulfilled by Him. He gave me everything that I looked so hard for in so many different areas of my life. He showed me love, affirmation, acceptance, and hope. He changed my heart and my life. God became everything I ever needed.

Second, I realized it was not necessarily that God removed that selfish purpose from within me, it was that He just *shifted* it to point to Him. Instead of caring so much about myself and my life, I began to care more about God and how I could use my life to glorify Him. No longer was my purpose to make my name known, but to make His name known. I was no longer living for me but for the God who lived in me. It really was that simple. My purpose in life changed from wanting to do everything I could for me, to wanting to do everything I could for God.

Radically different

That change in purpose is what caused my whole life to change, because I knew I could no longer live the way I had been living. It would be impossible. When we are born-again in Christ, the ways we think, act, and relate to others are completely transformed. We now live to glorify God and show people how amazing our God is by how we live our lives. And I believe the only way to show people Jesus through our way of living, is to live a *radically different* life.

I will unpack this idea of living "radically different," but I want to start off by sharing the story of when I first realized that living this way is what God has called every one of us to do.

Growing up "Christian," I didn't do certain things the other kids at my school would do. For example, while my friends went around cursing like it was no big deal, I would consciously refrain from uttering a single swear word because I knew God didn't create my mouth to speak in that way. While my friends constantly yelled at their parents and belittled them, I treated mine respectfully and kindly, because it was important to me that I honored them. And while my classmates would come to school every day tired and moody, I would come in each morning with a smile, because I knew it was my opportunity to glorify God.

In pretty much every aspect of my life, I just felt *different* from everybody else. I found it difficult to relate to people, and because of the reversed way I was living my life, I often heard comments like, "You're so not cool!" or, "You're so innocent." I hated when people called me those things. I hated that it was automatically "uncool" if I was against swearing, if I hugged my parents, or if I enjoyed school. It just didn't make any sense.

At first, I tried to brush it off and didn't let it get to me. I was confident that I was doing the right thing. But of course, as I kept hearing those comments more and more, I wondered if it was worth holding on to all these values. At the time, I was just in middle school and with everyone trying to fit in with the crowd, I was tired of being the "odd one out." There were many times I thought, *Maybe I should just be like them. Everyone else is doing all these things, I should just do them too!* I didn't want to be different. I just wanted to be like everybody else and do what everybody else was doing.

I remember coming home one day and complaining about all this to my dad. After I told him how I felt so different and excluded, I expected he would reassure me, affirm I wasn't different, and say it was all just in my head. But when I finished, he looked up at me and told me, "Izzy, you are different…" I rolled my eyes thinking, *Wow, thanks Dad. That's exactly what I wanted to hear.* But my dad continued by saying, "…because you *should* be different." *Wait what?* I asked my dad what he meant, and he told me, "You're a Christian. You should be different because God has made you *new.*"

I remember being so confused as I walked away from that conversation all those years ago. I had no idea what my dad was talking about. It was only after I experienced God for myself, and was transformed into a new creation, that I finally understood. Christians are supposed to be different, but not just different, *radically different!* Why? Because when we start living for God and carrying out His purpose for our lives, instead of our own, everything about what we do and how we live should change.

On fire for God

So, what exactly does that change look like? It looks *crazy.* Let me explain: One day as I was reading the Bible, I came across Romans 12:2 and it was like the verse highlighted itself right there in front of me. It says: "Do not be conformed to this world, but be transformed by the renewal of your mind, that by testing you may discern what is the will of God, what is good and

91

acceptable and perfect." This was a verse I had read so many times before, but that day, I could not stop looking at it. My eyes were fixed on the word *transform*.

I kept reading this verse repeatedly and felt like the Lord was trying to speak to me through that bit of Scripture. I eventually read it so many times that I memorized it, but I still couldn't quite figure out what the Lord was trying to tell me. After a good thirty minutes of just staring at that verse, I realized it was pretty late, so I was about to go to bed, when all of a sudden, I got a random urge to go on YouTube© (which is strange because I don't go on there often). I went on and the first video that popped up on my screen was of this girl named Emma Mae Jenkins.

Now if you don't know who Emma Jenkins is, she's basically a young social media influencer, author, speaker, and YouTuber whose sole purpose is to lead others into a relationship with Jesus (amazing, right?). However, I didn't know any of this when I saw her video pop up on my screen. In fact, I had never even heard of her. And usually, if I'm not too familiar with someone, I'll just scroll right past their video. But this time, something inside me told me to watch it.

So, I tapped on Emma's video, started watching, and was immediately drawn in by her contagious smile and fervent passion for Jesus. She started by talking simply about how much she loves God and how He gives her so much confidence, despite the lies the enemy might throw at her. She then said that her confidence helps her keep living out her purpose—to glorify

God in everything she does, even when people around her might not say the nicest things. She said it was because her purpose wasn't to please others, but to please *God.*

Honestly, by the middle of the video, I just started crying because I was so amazed and inspired by how much Emma exuded the love of Christ. The first thing she did in the morning was sing to the Lord, because she simply couldn't help herself. She loved God so much that she couldn't help spending every *waking moment* doing something for His glory. Even when it was just getting out of bed in the morning, she didn't take a single step until she prayed to God (over her *feet!*) that every step she took would be for Him and for her to live out His purpose for her that day. It was like nothing I had ever seen before. She was so unapologetically in love with Jesus and it was amazing to see.

After finishing the video, I scrolled down to read the comments, expecting to read stuff like "Your passion is contagious!" or, "I love how you love the Lord," or statements of that sort. But to my shock, what I found was the exact opposite. My jaw dropped. People said such terrible things like, "This girl is crazy," or, "She smiles way too much for a normal person." There were even people who commented, "She looks like she's on something." And as I was reading through all these hateful comments, not only was I in complete shock, but I also was angry and a little sad inside. Here was this beautiful and amazing girl simply sharing her passion for Jesus, and these people who commented just had to say all these negative things.

But as I was thinking this, Romans 12:2 popped into my mind again, and it was like a lightbulb went off. Everything clicked. I finally knew what the Lord was telling me. See, Emma Jenkins was *transformed*. She wasn't conforming to the world or what the world deemed "normal." No, she was overflowing with love, bursting with joy, and burning with passion. Why? Simply because of God! Simply because she saw it as a privilege every day to worship the One who had changed her life. She was a walking example of what someone who has been transformed by the love of God should look like. And the truth is, this kind of transformation often looks crazy to other people.

I looked back at that one comment, "She looks like she's on something," and that's when I realized, yes, *she is on something*. She is on *fire* for God. She is living in freedom. She is living her life in constant rejoice because of the goodness of the Lord. That's why she smiles so much. That's why she can't stop talking about Jesus. That's why she is so full of life and energy—because she has been *transformed*. And, to non-Christians, she looks crazy! All those who commented things like, "There's no way someone can be that happy," or, "How can anyone be that passionate?" wrote them because they didn't understand that Jesus just brings *that* much joy and excitement to a rather ordinary life!

Why am I telling you all this? Because I believe Emma Jenkins is an example of how we should all be living our lives—simply to love and glorify God. And if that is our purpose, we *should* look crazy to other people. We should! We should be overflowing with joy and happiness. We should be smiling every chance we get. We should be the evidence that God lives in us every single day.

Think about it. If we didn't live in this radically different way, how would anyone know we have found our happiness, joy, and peace in this amazing God? If we weren't radically different, how would anyone know their broken lives had the potential to be completely transformed? If we weren't radically different, how would anyone know Christianity isn't just a label but a whole new way of living? They would never know!

It's not only okay to be different, we have to be radically different. A radically different life results from a purpose to want to glorify God and show others His glory, no matter the cost. That is so present in Emma Mae Jenkins' life; she is an amazing example of someone living out their God-centered purpose.

But I want to talk about one other person, because there's someone more amazing who lived out this same purpose first. You might've heard of Him. His name is Jesus.

A radically different God

Jesus was the most radically different person to ever live. Everything He did was the opposite of what the world expected. Because of that, lots of people reacted to Jesus with hostility and jealousy—especially the

Pharisees. They couldn't understand Jesus' over-flowing love and compassion for other people. They couldn't understand why Jesus would wash His disciples' feet. They couldn't understand why Jesus would love the people who hurt Him the most. I'm sure a lot of people thought Jesus was crazy, but that didn't bother Jesus one bit. He knew He was the Way, the Truth, and the Life (John 14:6). He knew His Way was the right way, the better way, the more loving way. And the thing is, Jesus had to be *that* different from everybody else for people to see Him and realize how amazing *God* truly was.

When Jesus came to earth, He didn't live like the world expected Him to live. Not one bit. For example, instead of making a grand entrance with trumpets and big crowds, the King of the universe came down as a baby in a manger. Instead of acting like the all-powerful God He was and is, Jesus became completely human and faced all the temptations and sufferings we face. Instead of living the grand, royal life He very much deserved, Jesus dedicated the entirety of His life to serving us. Matthew 20:28 says, "The Son of Man did not come to be served, but to serve, and to give his life as a ransom for many."

Finally, instead of completing His life on earth and returning peacefully to His Father in Heaven, Jesus made the ultimate sacrifice of dying on the cross for our sins, so that we could spend an eternity in Heaven with God. Out of His abundant love for us, Jesus chose to pay the price for everything bad we had done. Jesus didn't live for power, fame, or wealth. Jesus lived to serve God through serving and loving us. That was His purpose. That's the radically different God we serve.

And since we serve a radically different God, it only makes sense that we should live with the same purpose Jesus had—to glorify God through loving and serving others. Philippians 2:5–8 even tells us: "In your relationships with one another, have the same mindset as Christ Jesus: Who, being in very nature God, did not consider equality with God something to be grasped, but made himself nothing, taking the very nature of a servant, being made in human likeness. And being found in appearance as a man, he humbled himself and became obedient to death—even death on a cross!"

Not easy, but worth it

The story and life of Jesus amazes me every time. He lived so differently from the rest of the world. He lived a life of humility, servant-heartedness, unconditional love, and self-sacrifice. He lived with a purpose, not for His personal fame nor gain, but for the God whom He loved with all His heart.

But it wasn't easy; living radically different never is. We saw that first in the story I shared at the beginning about me living differently because I was Christian. The way I was taught to live at a young age wasn't what the "norm" was. It was different and living differently clearly had its social consequences, and that was even before I truly met Christ! We saw it again with Emma Mae Jenkins, who shows us living for Jesus won't always get approval and praise from the outside world. In fact, it might have opposite responses and consequences, but she also shows us there's a far greater purpose than trying to please others, and a far greater reward than getting people's approval.

Finally, we saw it with Jesus—the ultimate example of a life lived radically different from the world. Jesus showed us what love looked like in a world that was, and still is, corrupt with greed and selfishness. He showed us what sacrifice looked like in a world that is still drenched in sin and evil. And because of Jesus' life and the purpose God fulfilled through His life, we now get to live our lives in relationship with our Father in Heaven. Because of Jesus' life, we now get to live in freedom from our sin. We can now have hope for eternity and purpose for the present.

Show them Jesus

Since accepting Christ, my mantra going into anything has been: "Show people Jesus." That has become my main purpose in life. And it's funny sometimes when people ask me about my big plan for my future or what my big dream is, because I'll always reply with the same answer: *I want to live a life so radically different that when people see me, they see Jesus. I just want to lead people to Him.*

Often, when I'm talking to unbelievers, many of them will criticize or question me, asking if that's *all* I want to do. And honestly, *yes, that's all I want to do,* because to me, there is nothing I can accomplish in this world that would be nearly as important or significant as leading people to Christ. While becoming an amazing volleyball player, or getting into a good college would give me temporary success and maybe validation in this lifetime, telling someone about God has the potential to affect another person's *salvation*. It has the potential to affect *eternity*, and that is, hands down, the most important thing I could ever do.

So, whether it's going to school every morning, to volleyball practice, or just walking around in the mall, my purpose is to show people Jesus. That doesn't mean I go up to everybody and tell them about God (although that is sometimes what we need to do!). It means I do my best to make sure my actions and words reflect God's character and love. It means I use the gifts God has given me, like being welcoming and inclusive, to reach out to more people. It means I use the platforms I have been given to set an example of what it means to live a life of love, of hope, and of Christ.

You can live out your purpose no matter what you're doing and no matter where you are. You don't have to be some pastor or missionary to show people Jesus. You can be a student at high school, just like me, and have that purpose. How? By doing what Christ would do—welcome the new student, sit with the kids who always sits by themselves at lunch, truly invest in and care about your friends, and radiate positivity wherever you go. You never know when those small things you do will lead to opportunities for you to tell somebody about the hope you have in Christ.

Unexpected opportunities

Let me tell you a story. It was around the middle of my sophomore year of high school. I was going to my classes as usual, when I noticed a new girl in class. The teacher announced she was a transfer student. Immediately, I got up and introduced myself to her. I welcomed her to the school, and became her first friend in a completely new environment. She was in two of my classes, which led us to talking more and more.

A few days later in our language arts class, the teacher asked us to discuss this article we were assigned with the person next to us. It just so happened that the teacher moved this new girl next to me for the discussion. I was super happy the teacher did that; It was my chance to get to her better and continue to make her feel welcome.

We talked and discussed the article, but after a few minutes, she stopped and looked up at me. I looked at her confused, wondering why she was looking at me like that, when she blurted, "What made you reach out to me? Why would you go out of your way to make me feel welcome?" At first, I didn't really know what to say, because that was just the kind of person God changed me to be. *But that was exactly it!* I had the willingness and capacity to reach out to this girl because of God. I immediately thought back to my mantra—*show people Jesus,* and I remembered I wanted my life to be the window through which people saw Jesus. So, I replied, "You know, it's because God changed my life."

After I told her that, she explained how she had gone to church growing up but stopped going when her parents stopped. She then shared with me pretty much her life story and explained how she had transferred to my school because of the extreme bullying to which she had fallen victim to at her old school. She had gone through depression, eating disorders, and just suffered through so much because of people who didn't treat her right. She was so vulnerable, but I sat and listened as she shared with me all the terrible things that had happened to her.

After she shared, she asked me if I could explain what I meant by God changing my life. I told her a little bit about my story and how I had gone through similar seasons of feeling depressed and alone. I told her how God lifted me out of the dark place I was in, and gave me so much happiness, joy, and life that I could never have received or gained from anything in this world. I told her that was why I now reached out to people and tried to make people feel welcome—to show people the love I first received from Jesus.

As I went on, I could see her face beaming; she was focusing so intently on what I was saying. She kept asking questions and asked me to tell her more, so I kept sharing with her. I also told her if she ever wanted to come with me to church, I would be more than happy to take her. She said she would love that.

I wanted to share this story because it shows how you can show Jesus anywhere and to anyone, if you know what your purpose is. Everywhere you look, there will be someone who needs somebody to show them the love of Christ, and our job as Christians is to be that somebody. Sometimes, showing someone God's love is simply reaching out to that person with kindness. To that person, we might represent the first time they experience the love and caring nature of God. That's the potential we all have, the potential to be the hands, touch, and love of God to the people around us. And who knows? One day, maybe that girl to whom I witnessed might remember what I said and accept Christ into her life.

No in-between

I wanted to wrap up this chapter by sharing one of my favorite quotes. It's by C.S. Lewis (1898-1963) and is:

> *Christianity, if false, is of no importance, and if true, of infinite importance, the only thing it cannot be is moderately important.*[1]

Now, you're probably wondering what this quote has to do with finding your purpose, so let me explain.

I'm sharing this quote because I have met people who have said things to me like, "Yes, I believe in God

---

[1] "C. S. Lewis Quotes." BrainyQuote.com. BrainyMedia Inc, 2021. 24 February 2021.
https://www.brainyquote.com/quotes/c_s_lewis_164517

and have accepted Him into my life. But I mean, having God be at the center and purpose of my life? That's a little much. He's just part of my life, that's all." If you're someone who thinks like this, you're not alone. A lot of us, if not most of us, treat Christianity as though it is moderately important at best. Many of us say we believe in the faith, but we don't really live it out or incorporate it into anything we do. Our lives would be the same whether we were "Christian" or not, so our purpose and goals in life are not centered around Christ, but are centered around something we believe is more important than Christ.

Now, if those thoughts sound familiar, I want to challenge you to consider what I'm about to say, because here's the thing: If you believe Jesus *died for your sins and rose from the dead* so that you could have a *relationship with Him* and have the *gift of eternal life with God* in Heaven; if you believe Jesus *split* the sea; performed countless *miracles*; promised to *always be with you*, *protect you,* and *unconditionally love you*, then Christianity cannot just be moderately important to you. It just can't.

We have a God who sent His Son to die for us. We have a God who loved us while we were still sinners. We have a God who wants us and has a plan for us. We have a God who will never leave our side. If we really understand the magnitude of that, and believe these truths for ourselves, our lives should be radically different. I'd go even further and say our lives should be radically *transformed*, because our God is *not* just a moderately important God.

I believe there is only one type of Christian and that is a *radically different* Christian. There is no in-between, because the truth is, if God is real, and if we claim to believe all that the Bible says, then our faith should be nothing short of the most important and dominant thing in our lives. That also means our purpose should be centered around glorifying God and letting everyone know about this amazing God we believe in and love.

When you find God, you find purpose. It's as simple as that. When you fully embrace who God is and what that means for your life, it will be impossible for you to want to do anything else with your life than to live it for God. He is infinitely important, above anything else in this world, and over anything we can accomplish. There's a quote hanging in my room that I read in, *New Morning Mercies: A Daily Gospel Devotional* (P. D. Tripp, 2014, Crossway) and it says, "If you're God's child, the gospel isn't an aspect of your life, *it is your life*; that is, it is the window through which you look at everything."

I love that quote. The gospel *is* our life. *God is our life,* and when God is our life, God becomes our purpose. When God becomes our purpose, we start living a radically different life. And when people look at our radically different lives, they'll see Jesus.

6

Finding Passion

"What makes you so passionate?"

During my middle school and early high school years, I remember being asked so many times, "What are you passionate about?" Whether it was a question on some application I had to fill out, or something a friend or teacher asked me, this question seemed to come up a lot in my everyday life. And I hated it, I really hated that question. Why? Because whenever that question came up, the conversation always went a little something like this:

Friend: "So, what are you passionate about?"

Me: "Um, well you know, uh, that thing... uh, well actually I don't know"

Friend: "What do you mean you don't know? I'm just asking what some things are in life you care a lot about."

Me: "Uh, I guess volleyball? I don't really know; I don't really have much interest in anything other than that"

Friend: "Oh, um I meant like more important stuff. Like what are some issues that you feel passionate about? Personally, I really care about protecting the environment."

Me: "That's great! I'm glad you're passionate about the environment. Uh, for me, I'm not sure. I mean, obviously I care about stuff and, like, the issues that our world is facing and all that, but I don't really have anything I'd say I'm *passionate* about."

Friend: "Oh, so do you not, like, want to be part of the change or help change the world?"

Me: "Um, I mean it would be great if the world changes, but yeah, I don't really have a desire to change the world. It's not really my business anyway, other people who are more passionate than me should work on that stuff."

Friend: "Oh, ok" (probably thinking I was some heartless person who didn't have an ounce of motivation to care about something bigger than herself).

Which, unfortunately, was pretty much true. That's how all conversations dealing with passion went for me. As sad and messed up as it was, I just didn't really care about the things going on in the world. I didn't necessarily care about the problems right in front of me, and even when I heard or knew about people in the world who were suffering, I didn't pay much attention to it. Nothing seemed to be bad enough or convicting enough to care about or feel compassion about in my heart. It was as if my heart was made of stone; nothing could move me.

With that said, it wasn't as if I didn't want to care, or was trying not to care. I had always been envious of passionate people who did all these things to help make a change. Those people inspired me; I so desperately wanted to love and care about the world and people as much as they did, but I just couldn't. I couldn't find passion or love in my heart.

But here's the thing about passion; it can only come from a place of love. For me, the problem was that there wasn't a lot of love in my heart. As I explained in Chapter 1, years of being closed-off and blocking out people from my life led to lots of bitterness and coldness within me. I lost countless friends and important people during that season and was left with very few genuine relationships. When time goes on without having close relationships to people like your friends and your siblings, it lessens the amount of love you feel in your heart. Because I wasn't pouring out love, or receiving love from certain relationships, I lacked love for myself. Looking back, I think it was my inability to love myself that prevented me from loving others and the world. I just didn't have the capacity to feel passion and care about other things when I lacked any foundation of love toward myself to begin with.

A relationship with God

What I found when I formed a relationship with God was that He was my foundation of love. When God showed me who I was to Him, and showed me that I was worthy of love, I began having the capacity to feel passion and care about people and things outside of myself. As I continued getting to know God more through His Word and through prayer, I found myself caring a lot about the things God loved and disliking the things that weren't pleasing to God. It was through God, and knowing what He was passionate about, that I found my passions.

What I mean is, imagine you're reading an article or watching the news and you hear that there has been an increase in gang violence in a neighborhood near you. Naturally, the most important and urgent part of this news is the *near you* part. You are completely alarmed and even scared, so you do some more research, but when you do further research, you realize the neighborhood with the increase in gang violence is not so near you after all. In fact, it happens to be far enough away that it won't be a problem to you or your family. Immediately, you're relieved. You stop worrying and continue with whatever you were doing.

A few days later, you meet with one of your best friends, and this friend tells you they lost everything and have to move. When you ask your friend where they are moving, she says the name of the neighborhood with the increase in gang violence that you just read about. Right away, you tell your friend the news about the neighborhood, but she tells you she has no other choice; that neighborhood is the only place she can afford. You give her a worried look, but she comforts you and tells you that everything will be alright.

A month goes by and your friend seems to be doing fine. You keep meeting up with her every week and things couldn't be better. Then, you get a call from the police and they tell you your best friend was badly beaten by a gang in her area. Immediately, you boil with anger and drive as quickly as you can to see your friend. When you see the scars on your best friend's face, your heart breaks for her and you start weeping.

As soon as you come back home, you start researching and educating yourself about these gangs in your friend's neighborhood. You even donate a large amount of money toward helping the victims of the violence, and you tell everybody how terrible the gang violence in that area really is.

You develop a deep passion for caring about the gang violence in the area, because now it's no longer just some area far away from you, but it's an area where your best friend was so badly hurt. Because of your relationship with that friend, her struggles and pain are now your struggles and pain. And because you know that gang activity has caused your best friend pain, you want to do everything you can to help fight against it and protect the people in that area.

The point of this example is to show you that sometimes you need to have a personal relationship with someone for their struggle to matter to you. At times, it may not matter how bad something seems on the news or in an article, if it doesn't have any relevance to you. Like in the example above, hearing about the increase in gang violence in a faraway neighborhood might not be that important to you until your best friend gets hurt because of it. Often, genuine passion stems from a relationship—a relationship you care so much about that you care about whatever the person in the relationship cares about.

Since I didn't have many relationships I genuinely cared about, I had a hard time caring about other things. Nothing seemed to be relevant or important enough for me to be passionate about it. But that changed when I formed a relationship with God.

When I met God and started to learn all about Him through reading His Word and in prayer, I grew close to Him, just like I would with any other relationship. But this relationship was one I loved with all my heart. And because I loved God so much, I started loving the things He loved. For example, Psalm 34:18 says, "The LORD is near to the brokenhearted and saves the crushed in spirit." When I first learned that about God, I also began to care for the brokenhearted and crushed in spirit. I knew those people were where God's heart was, and because God loved those people, I wanted to love them, too, because now they had relevance, and was importance to me. Why? Because they were important to God. Countless Bible verses state how God dislikes it when His people don't love and do good to the broken and crushed, and how God wants us to love those who hate us, bless those who curse us, and pray for those who abuse us (Luke 6:27–28). God states clearly in 1 John 3:17 that if any of us see our brothers and sisters in need, and yet close our hearts against them, His love cannot abide in us.

So, it was through forming a relationship with God that I found my passion for the world and people around me. It was through coming to know what's important to God, what God loves, and who God loves that I could care about those same things and people. This was how I found my passion—through that one, crucial relationship. I learned that unless you have a personal relationship with God, the things important to Him will not be important to you. Maybe you're like me and feel you lack passion. Maybe you find it hard to recognize relevance and importance in things because they don't apply to you or affect you. Maybe you never had a reason to care.

Well, now you do—because God cares. He cares about all the problems going on in the world. He cares about those in poverty, those stuck in war-torn countries, those struggling with mental illness, and those crushed in spirit. Maybe you've known about all these problems, but they never became that important to you. They had never been important to me either, but suddenly, they became incredibly important. I realized all the problems and struggles in the world had every bit of relevance to me. Every person in the world who is struggling, is a child of God, just like you and me. Every person was knitted together in their mother's womb and is so precious to Him. Once I had a relationship with God, all those problems and struggles to which I had previously turned a blind eye, became my problems and struggles. God's pain was now my pain. His passions were now my passions.

Finding your passion

However, just because God's passion is now your passion, doesn't mean you have to pour into and fight for everything God fights for. That would be impossible for us to do alone. That's why God created all types of different people. He wired and formed each of us with certain interests and callings so we could wholeheartedly pursue specific things. Although each of our passions may differ, each passion is fueled by our relationship with Jesus. Our first passion for Jesus allows us to be passionate for His people and His world.

My passion for youth

For me, I was drawn to God's passion for the youth. One of my favorite verses is 1 Timothy 4:12: "Don't let anyone look down on you because you are young, but set an example for the believers in speech, in conduct, in love, in faith and in purity." When I first read that verse, I was strongly convicted in my heart, and as I read other verses about God's hope and love for the youth, I developed a deep passion for teenagers and their potential to change the world through faith. Another Scripture passage I often return to is Jeremiah 1:4–8 which says: "Now the word of the LORD came to me, saying, 'Before I formed you in the womb, I knew you, and before you were born, I consecrated you; I appointed you a prophet to the nations.' Then I said, 'Ah, Lord God! behold, I do not know how to speak, for I am only a youth.' But the Lord said to me, 'Do not say, "I am only a youth"; for to all to whom I send you, you shall go, and whatever I command you, you shall speak. Do not be afraid of them, for I am with you to deliver you, declares the LORD.'"

It was through these verses that I felt God calling me to pursue this passion of His. In these verses and many more, it's clear that God believes in us as teenagers to set an example for believers by how we live our lives with love and faith. It's clear God believes our youthfulness, which society too often deems immaturity and lack of readiness, is not something to look down on. No, instead, God calls us teenagers to *go,* He calls us to not be afraid, but to trust and obey Him.

Because I know what God says about us is the truth, it breaks my heart when I see my peers and friends discouraged and feeling a lack of purpose. It breaks my heart when I see teenagers around me who feel like they aren't enough, or they can't do anything because they are young. It just breaks my heart because I know God could use them in radical and extraordinary ways, if they just put their faith in Him.

And honestly, this was one of the first times my heart really broke. I used to never be moved; nothing ever used to be enough to break me, but this did. So, I decided I wanted to pursue this passion with my life. I not only want to see my generation saved, but I also want to see it transformed. I want to see youth live lives in which God is glorified and made known to the whole world.

My inspirational friend

Something I've learned is that when you pursue a passion fueled by your passion for God, crazy things will happen. They really will. Let me tell you a story about one of my best friends, Nathan Lee. I met Nathan just half a year ago when his family moved here to Washington from California, because his dad became our new senior pastor. But something crazy happened before he made the move.

See, Nathan also had a passion for seeing His generation saved, fueled by his love for God. Before he left California for good, he talked to some leaders at his school and asked them if he could give a message to the students during his last lunch period there. He wanted nothing more than to preach the gospel to his peers before he left. Even though he had never spoken in front of such a big audience, and was probably extremely nervous to speak about something that not many believed, his passion for Jesus and youth gave him courage. When that day came, Nathan bravely and boldly went in front of the student body, trusted that

God would speak through him, and preached about the love of Jesus. He stood proudly and unashamedly as he proclaimed the truth of the gospel to hundreds of students. He poured out his heart and shared vulnerably about his testimony, how God had turned his life around. And this is a sixteen-year-old we are talking about! But this sixteen-year-old was so fired up with his passion and zeal for God that God was able to work radically and extraordinarily through him. At the end of his message, he blessed all the students and prayed they would all come to know Jesus one day. And because of Nathan's confident passion, God showed up in that school in an amazing way. That day, eleven students came up to Nathan and chose to give their lives to Jesus. How incredible is that?

That's the power of passion. Passion for God leads to action from God, and that day, God used Nathan to save the lives of eleven of his peers as well as introduce the name of Jesus to every single student listening to him. And the thing is, he wasn't some pastor or missionary, or even an educated adult. He was a youth, a teenager. He didn't have experience or a wealth of knowledge, but he had passion. And since Jesus fueled that passion, God was able to do crazy things.

Becoming a writer

It was hearing about and witnessing stories like these, in which God worked in amazing ways through teen-agers, that grew my passion bigger and bigger. I wanted every teenager to know that God could do amazing things through their lives, if they just had faith in Him.

One evening, I met with Pastor Esther at a coffee shop and I remember telling her about this passion of mine. I remember going on and on about how I just wanted teenagers to know God, and how I wanted to share and witness to them how He changed my life and how He could change theirs. As I was talking, I felt like I could go on and on—that was the cool part. I had never been able to go on and on about anything, mainly because I never had anything I was passionate enough to go on and on about. But this time, I couldn't stop talking.

After I finished explaining my desire, Pastor Esther looked me straight in the eye and asked me if I had ever considered writing a book. My first instinct was to laugh. *That's funny*, was the first thought that came to mind, but when I realized she was being serious, I stopped laughing. No way had I ever thought about it! I then told her about my awful history with writing.

See, language arts had always been my weakest class. I couldn't write for my life. I vividly remember every single essay I had to write for school and literally locking myself in my room to write each one of them. In my room, I would hopelessly stare at the blank word document in front me, dreading having to spend the next few days trying to write an essay. And the thing is, I was a hardcore perfectionist, so I couldn't move onto writing another sentence until the sentence I was writing was perfect. Everything had to flow nicely, have the right vocabulary worlds and, to put it simply, be *flawless*. So, as you can probably imagine, it took me an incredibly long time to even write a few sentences, let alone a whole essay. What's worse was when I finally overcame my insane writer's block and lack of creative ideas and actually wrote the paper, I would read it over, realize it was terrible, and delete the entire thing. Why did I delete the entire thing? Because I was so much of a perfectionist that I couldn't just delete or fix one section, I had to start again from scratch. So, with tears pouring from my eyes, I would once again start the excruciating process of writing my essay.

For that very reason, when Pastor Esther asked me if I had ever considered writing a *book*, I said definitely not. *I mean, that's like one hundred essays, right? Yeah, no thank you. I couldn't even write one essay without almost dying in the process. A whole book? That was unheard of.* But Pastor Esther insisted that I should at least try journaling some of my thoughts, so with much persuasion and encouragement, I bought a notebook and started writing. I was hesitant at first because I had tried journaling several times when I was younger but failed miserably—again because of my perfectionist tendencies, but also because I just could never think of anything to write.

But when I journaled this time, it was like the pages wrote themselves. The passion and fire God ignited in my soul filled the pages of my notebook with all the things I wanted to say to others about God's amazing love. I realized I now had so many things I *wanted* to write about. I wasn't thinking about making each sentence perfect or making sure my vocabulary words were advanced enough. I was simply writing from my heart.

Before long, I graduated from my notebook and moved on to my computer. My thoughts became way too fast for my hand to catch up, so the change from pencil to keys was necessary. As I kept finding inspiration and passion to write, I realized maybe Pastor Esther's suggestion to write a book wasn't such a far-fetched idea after all. Maybe this was my way of telling people about Jesus. Maybe this was how I would reach and inspire teenagers. Maybe my writing and experiences could lead someone to Jesus.

So, I started writing the first drafts of the book you are now holding in your hands and honestly, it's simply crazy. Writing a book was not something I had ever planned to do, but now writing is something I love doing. I guess it just goes to show how God can do crazy and unexpected things in and through your life when you are overflowing with passion for Him.

When you love Jesus and are on fire for Him, nothing is impossible. Passion for Jesus has the power to break odds and allow God to enter and do things in your life that you may have never dreamed of.

Remind me, Lord

Until this point, I've talked about how I found passion and how passion can lead to God doing amazing things, but I also wanted to talk about what I do when that passion dies down. Although it would be ideal if we could stay on fire for God every single moment of every day, the reality is, we are all sinners; there *will* be times when we lose sight of God and lose sight of the passion we once had for Him.

To be honest, when I first met God, I didn't think that was possible. I was so on fire for Jesus and wanting to do everything for Him, that losing my passion for Him was not even a thought or concern in my mind. And for a while, I didn't lose it. I lived my best life, full of the happiness and joy I found through Jesus, doing everything I could to make His name known. I was immersing myself in His Word and prayer. The Holy Spirit was constantly filling me and I finally found an amazing community at church, involving myself in many of their weekly hangouts and gatherings. My relationships with people dramatically improved as I was becoming a better friend, a more loving sister, and a kinder stranger. Everything was going well—until COVID-19 hit.

Suddenly, everything was turned upside down. I couldn't hang out with my friends or go to school anymore, but most important, I couldn't go to church. That was the worst. No church meant no youth hangouts or weekly worship nights. Those were the events I had looked forward to at the end of every week. Those were the events that would fill me and remind me of God's goodness and faithfulness.

As I look back, I'm realizing maybe it was from those events that I was drawing most of my passion, so without these events every week, I saw myself falling into a spiritual slump. As I reflected, I realized how much I depended on *people* to make me feel God's presence. I realized it was a whole lot *easier* to feel God when you were surrounded by your friends at church. It was a whole lot *easier* to feel God when you had a band in the room playing powerful worship music. It was a whole lot *easier* to feel God when your pastor was leading you through prayer and Scripture. And just like it was a lot easier to feel God when all those things were present, it was also a lot easier for me to maintain my passion and fire for Him when I was constantly in that environment.

I found it was a lot harder to feel God when I was stuck at home by myself in my room. I didn't quite know what to do with myself. I figured that everything would just blow over soon, so during the first few weeks of quarantine, I'll admit I wasted a lot of time. I watched a ton of movies, slept a lot, and scrolled through Instagram a few times too many.

I knew I should've been reading the Bible or spending time in prayer instead, but I kept pushing it aside. I told myself I would just do it later, but as we all know, later usually means never. I just couldn't find any motivation to set aside a few hours to talk to God. It was only a matter of days before I felt empty inside. I was experiencing some of those terrible feelings I thought I would never feel again since meeting Christ. I was feeling lonely and almost hopeless. I saw myself getting easily irritated with my family, and I was constantly stressed over every little thing. Finally, things were so rock bottom that I told myself I needed to go back to Jesus.

Binging Netflix© was not going to work this time, watching YouTube© for hours was not going to rid me of my loneliness, and wasting my time on Instagram© was not going to help me with my feelings of hopelessness. So, I went into my room, shut the door, turned off the lights, and fell to my knees.

As I was on my knees, I cried and just prayed to God. It was a desperate prayer. I had no intention of trying to do a half-hearted prayer and getting back to my lazy day. I also had no feelings of being rushed into finishing up quickly. I knew, at that moment, I needed God more than anything. Minutes turned to hours and before I knew it, it was 1a.m. in the morning. I was on the floor weeping, just asking God to let me feel His presence. I asked Him to remind me of the time when I first felt His love back at summer camp and to let me feel it again. And as I was praying these things to God, I felt His peace cover me. I sat there on the ground simply enjoying being in the presence of God.

After feeling fully satisfied in my heart, I got up from my knees and walked toward my bed to go to sleep for the night, when I suddenly felt God prompting me to go play the piano. In my head, I was thinking, *Um, God it's a little late for that, don't You think?* But nevertheless, I went to the mini electric piano in the corner of my room, sat down, and started playing some simple chords. Immediately, the words of the prayer I had just prayed all night kept popping into my mind. I started singing my prayer along with the chords, and it felt like God was telling me to make a song out of it. So that's what I did. Here are the lyrics:

Lord, I need You
I need to hear Your voice
I need to feel Your love
I need to be in Your presence

'Cause at times I feel lost and alone
Sometimes the darkness comes and tries to take hold
of me
And it feels like I'm just so far away
From where I used to be
That day You changed me

Remind me of the time when I first felt Your love
Remind me of the moment when I just stood in awe
of You
Remind me of Your grace and of Your love and of
Your promises
Oh, God, remind of Your love

My heart may wander
My mind may sway
But Your love is true and stays the same
From the moment I met You
To this very day

You have and will always remain

So even if I feel lost and alone
And if the darkness comes and tries to take hold of
me
And if it feels like I'm just so far away
From where I used to be
Where I still can be

Remind me of the time when I first felt Your love
Remind me of the moment when I just stood in awe
of You
Remind me of Your grace and of Your love and of
Your promises
Oh, God, remind me of Your love

Sometimes, to regain our passion, we just need to remind ourselves of all God has done for us and how much love He has shown us in the past. We need to remember our God is constant and never-changing, unlike our emotions and passions. Whether we feel on fire for Him or not, God is still God, and He is still working in our lives.

Running after You

Sometimes, when we think about being passionate for God, we forget God is also extremely passionate about us. But unlike our passion, God's passion is constant. And because of His overflowing passion for you, He won't let you lose your passion for Him so easily. As it says in the song *Goodness of God©*, by Bethel Music (2019), God's goodness is running after you. Always. Even when you lose sight of God and your passion fades, God never loses sight of you; He continues to love you no matter how far you fall away from Him.

I once heard an amazing analogy from a pastor named Will Chung. During one of his messages, Pastor Will had a baby monitor in his hand. On the screen of the monitor, his baby girl was sleeping soundly. He said he would constantly watch his daughter on the screen, and if she ever made even the slightest cry or called for her daddy, he would come running to her. He compared this to what God does for us when we call out to Him. He comes *running* to us. That's how much He loves us. That's how *passionate* He is about us.

That's the hope we can have. Even when we feel far from God, or we feel like we've lost our fire for Him, He hasn't lost His fire for us. So now, on those nights when I feel like I've drifted away from God, I go straight to my knees and ask God to remind me of His love for me. And the amazing thing about God is that when you choose to go running back to Him, He will already be waiting for you. He has been waiting for you, because nothing you do can make God lose His passion and love for you.

7

Finding Humility

"Where does your humility come from?"

Pride was the one sin I felt like I just couldn't overcome. It wasn't like selfishness, lying or cheating, which were all things I could intentionally avoid and work on to improve. It was much deeper and much more complex a problem than that. Pride, for me, was a heart problem, and it showed its ugly face in almost everything I did and even everything I thought about.

For example, whenever I was doing something good for the community, like serving or helping in some way, the first thought that came to mind would be, *I'm such a good person for doing this*. Or when I got rejected from something I applied for, my first thought would be, *Well, I deserve better anyway.* No matter what I was doing, prideful thoughts were the first thoughts to enter my mind. It was never, *Oh, I'm doing this because I just want to help,* or *this happened because I didn't work as hard as I should have.* It was always *I'm doing this because I'm an amazing person,* and *I got rejected because they don't know how to choose the right people.*

To put it simply, I thought very highly of myself. I thought I was better than other people. I thought I deserved better than the people around me. I thought nothing was ever my fault. I was arrogant. I was *prideful.* And my prideful attitude hurt me in many aspects of my life—mainly in my relationships with friends.

Ruined friendships

Friendships are hard. They're even harder when you're prideful and have the mindset that you're better than your friend. Such was the case for me. I couldn't keep a friend longer than a year, at most. And it was because my pride always got in the way sometime during all my friendships.

Let me tell you what I mean. I was proud of many things I did. I was proud that I was a good student with all A's and always did well on my tests. I was proud I was on the varsity volleyball team. I was proud of the compliments and comments I got from people because of my performance in the sport. I was very proud. Don't get me wrong, it's a good thing to be proud of yourself, but my proudness didn't just stop at that. It built up and up until it became sinful pride, and once my proudness turned into pride, it wasn't so good anymore.

All the things I was proud about myself not only led me to think very highly of myself, but it also led me to think less well of other people. I walked into my classes with an arrogant attitude, and I walked down the halls of my school with a feeling of superiority, as if getting good grades and being a good athlete somehow made be "better" and "more deserving" than the average student.

When I attempted making friends, I chose people I thought were at the "same level" as I was. I looked for people who were also talented athletes and smart. But even when I gained a friend who met the expectations I had set in my mind for them, I still had this feeling of superiority. I felt that somehow, me just being me should make *them* feel lucky or grateful that I was talking to them or wanting to be friends with them. I wanted them to know how *great* a person I was, and how many *great* things I had accomplished.

But, of course, going into a friendship with that sort of mindset would never produce any sort of stable and loving foundation that friendships must be birthed from. And so, all my friendships were short-lived. This was because whenever one of my friends did something to me that I thought was "mean," or just something I didn't like, my pride would get all riled up and I would immediately cut them out of my life. I didn't really believe in things like second chances or benefit of the doubt. Whenever any of my friends messed up in some way, I would be done with them. I would tell myself things like, *I don't need them. I deserve a much better friend than that. I didn't do anything wrong, and they had the nerve to say that to me? Ridiculous. I'm never talking to them again.*

And just like that, I'd be finished with that friend. Crazy and petty as it sounds, I wouldn't even give that friend a second thought. It didn't matter if we were friends for a day or for a year, I had so much pride in my heart that *I* had to be the one to leave them and make them feel like I never really cared for them anyway.

I vividly remember one friend I made in the eighth grade. We became close quickly and would hang out all the time outside of school. Looking back, I'd say I genuinely cared for this person. He was someone I enjoyed having as a friend, so much so that this friendship lasted until the end of my freshman year of high school. Now, you're probably thinking, *that was not very long, girl, that was only two years.* But hey! That was longer than most of my friendships, sad as it was.

Anyway, during the end of our freshman year, we got into a small argument, so small that I don't remember in the slightest what we argued about. But back then, in the heat of the moment, I remember telling my friend that I was done with him. I told him I was done talking to him, and from that point on, I cut him out of my life. I didn't wave to him in the hall like I used to, I didn't talk to him in class like I used to, and I didn't even acknowledge his presence in a room like I should have. That was how much my pride got in the way.

My pride told me the friendship didn't work out because *he* was a bad friend. My pride told me that the reason things spiraled downward the way they did was because *he* messed up. It was all *his* fault. In my mind, he was this terrible person who didn't deserve my friendship, while I thought I was this perfect friend who deserved so much more than his friendship. I believed I did nothing wrong or bad that could've contributed to the breakup.

This mindset led to me losing many of my friends. And it was not because we had arguments, and neither was it that my friend messed up sometimes. It was that I had so much *pride*, that I couldn't keep being friends with someone if I felt like they had wronged me in any way. I couldn't let the small stuff go and give my friend the benefit of the doubt. I wanted the other person in the friendship to regret what they did and watch me go on to meet "better" friends.

The log in my eye

I think the biggest thing God has taught me about humility in friendships is to reflect on what kind of friend *I* am being. My whole life, I wasted all my energy focusing on what kind of person my *friend* was. I kept nitpicking all the little things I didn't like about *them* and always looked for ways *they* could improve. I always thought all our problems stemmed from *them* being a bad friend, messing up, and *them* needing to get better.

I never stopped to think how *I* wasn't being the best friend and the things *I* could be better at.

I love what it says in Matthew 7:3: "Why do you see the speck that is in your brother's eye, but do not notice the log that is in your own eye?" This verse could not be more accurate. So many times, we fail to see what we need to work on ourselves, and where we might've messed up, because we are so focused on trying to pinpoint the trivial flaw we see in our friend. We become ignorant to all our own problems.

When I cut things off with the friend I mentioned earlier, my thoughts were filled with all the things my friend did wrong. I tried going down the list of the times he messed up and all the things I never liked about him, but in hindsight, as I reflect on the kind of friend I was to him, I'm realizing there were a lot of things I did wrong and could've done much better as well. In fact, as I look back, I probably messed up more than he ever did. I could've been more patient, forgiving, understanding, and the list goes on. But at the time of our friendship, my pride wouldn't let me humble myself to admit any of those things.

Self-reflection takes humility. Self-reflection takes understanding there are things about you that aren't great. It takes realizing there may be things you are doing that you don't even know are hurting your friendships. It takes acknowledging you might have messed up, and realizing what you did might've hurt your friend. But during that time of my life, I didn't have the humility either to admit or realize the things I might've done wrong.

A humble heart

When I found Jesus, He revealed to me my sin. He revealed to me how broken and messed up I really was. He showed me the log that was in my eye, and that log for me was my prideful, unforgiving heart.

Once I became aware of this log, I spent a lot of time in self-reflection. I reflected over all my current friendships and all the friendships that had been broken, and I saw the areas where I had messed up and needed improvement. I realized maybe *I* was the problem and it was never truly any of my friends' faults, but my lack of awareness of the harm I was causing.

That realization marked the day when I started walking into all my current friendships with a humble heart, knowing I needed to be better. I knew there were many areas I needed to work on in all my friendships, so I put that responsibility on myself to become better. I asked my friends how I could be better for them. I realized how I was contributing to conflicts, instead of automatically assuming it was my friend's fault. And I learned to be understanding and forgiving, even when it was my friend who might've messed up, because I knew there was always something I could've done differently as well.

As for all my friendships I had broken, I went back to reconcile with each of those friends after deep reflection on the kind of friend I was to them. After realizing the areas where I had screwed up, I admitted those things to my friends and told them I was sorry for how I hurt them. I'm not going to lie, it wasn't easy to stand before friends I had cut out of my life to tell them I messed up, and it was not easy to acknowledge and admit all the things I did wrong. But it was ever so necessary, and because I found the humility to find reconciliation, I'm now on good terms with all those people I had once cut out.

Since then, my friendships with people have been so much better and healthier because I went into them knowing I wasn't perfect, and neither was my friend. I went into them knowing I was flawed and broken, and I wouldn't always be the best friend. This simple mindset of humbleness in realizing I can always improve and be better for my friend has helped tremendously in my friendships, and even in my relationship with Jesus.

Humility in Jesus

Following Jesus requires humility. There's no way you can follow Him without it, because when you find God, you realize who He is compared to who you are. When I first realized exactly who God was, there was no way I could think of myself so highly anymore. Because even though I might've been a straight A student and a varsity volleyball player, God was the King of this universe, and if you ask me, that's not even a comparison.

It's humbling to realize you are just a small part of this amazing world God has created. It's humbling to understand your life here on earth is not only short, but is also just a blip in what has happened and what is yet to come. When I finally understood there was a much greater picture and a much greater God than just my life, I realized if my life wasn't to live for God, then it wasn't a life worth living. If what I was doing every day wasn't for God, then there was no point in doing it.

About a year ago, when I first started writing this book, I knew I was doing it for the sole purpose of making God's name known to the world. I wanted this book to be all for God since it was only because of God that I could even write it in the first place. So, in a place of humility and obedience toward God, I embarked on the journey of writing this book.

But at some time during this writing process, I shifted my focus off God and onto myself. Feelings of uninvited pride and selfishness crept into my heart, telling me to write this book to make *my name* known, instead. Pride and selfishness told me I should get the glory from writing it, and all this would be to make people *like me* and *know me*, instead of coming to know Jesus.

Suddenly, I was thinking thoughts like, *Wow, look at me. I'm writing my own book! Everyone will probably think I'm so amazing for doing this.* My mind crept into these selfish thoughts acknowledging *my work*, instead of acknowledging this work was all for *Jesus*, because of *Jesus*, and only done through *Jesus*. During this time of temptation, I was so caught up with being proud of myself that I forgot about all those years I spent living in brokenness and loneliness because I didn't know *God*. I forgot that it was *God* who saved me that night and changed my life forever. I forgot this dream to write a book was a dream *God* placed in me. And I forgot why I started this long process of writing a book in the first place—to share about how amazing *God* is.

When I reminded myself of who God is and the amazing work He had done in my life, I remember sitting on my bed and ripping up all the writing I had done that week that had been written with the mindset that it was for me. That day, I declared to myself that the dreams God gives me and the things God calls me to do will always be to make *His* name known, not my own. I was tired of the devil tempting me to believe that somehow, I was better than God. I was tired of him making me think that everything happening in my life was because of my works and my talent. I was tired of him making me want to follow the world's view of success and fame by trying to make a name for myself, rather than follow the One who gave me my name.

I remember so clearly the day when this realization hit. Right after I ripped up my writing, declared God's name was higher than mine would ever be, and chose humility over the devil's temptation, I sat up in my bed and looked straight into the mirror in my room. This mirror sat right above my dresser, and it was something I looked into every time I got up from bed.

But that day, when I looked into that mirror, something didn't feel right. As I looked into this mirror, all I saw was my arrogant, prideful, and easily tempted self. I saw a girl who sometimes thought she was better than God. I saw a girl who secretly desired to make her name known to the world. And that frustrated me. Mirrors reflect the person looking into them, but in that moment, the mirror didn't reflect what I wanted to see, nor what I wanted people to see in me.

I wanted my mirror and my life to reflect my amazing God. When I began thinking that as I looked into this mirror, the song lyrics from "More Like Jesus" by Passion, *if more of you means less of me, take everything*[2] suddenly came to mind. So, I took those lyrics and applied them literally in that situation to find out what less of me would really look like.

I cut out paper squares and laid them next to each other to try to make the shape of a large poster. I then wrote this message on it:

Izzy, it's not about you. It never was and never will be about you. The dreams God gives you are always for others. God's dreams are for His purposes and His people. God sent His Son to die for you. All the praise, honor and glory go to Him and Him alone. Dedicate your life to loving God and serving others just like Jesus did. Dedicate your life to your family, friends, and enemies. Let everything you do be for making

[2] Passion Conferences. (2018). "More Like Jesus." K. Stanfill. Whole Heart [Audio file]. Retrieved from https://music.apple.com/us/album/more-like-jesus-feat-kristian-stanfill-live/1440892028?i=1440892347

His name known, not your own. May you simply be the window through which people see the glory of God. Be a mirror of Jesus.

Once I wrote that, I picked up all the papers and brought them to the mirror in my room. I took each paper individually and taped it onto my mirror, and every time I taped one paper, it would cover a part of my reflection. As I kept going, more and more of me disappeared in the mirror as more and more of this message I wrote covered the mirror's surface. By the time I taped on the last paper, I could no longer see myself in the mirror, but what I did see was the full message of my declaration to Jesus.

In that moment, I thought about those lyrics again: *If more of you means less of me take everything,* and right then, I understood exactly what it meant. I wanted more of Jesus and I wanted my life to reflect Jesus (symbolized by me covering my mirror with paper). But that came with the cost of making there become less of me (symbolized with more and more of me being covered as I kept putting up papers). But if that meant there would be more of Jesus, I was okay with losing everything about me, and finally the whole mirror was covered to where I only saw Jesus. When I looked back into the mirror, I realized the feeling of unsettledness was gone. My mirror now reflected what I wanted myself and people to see.

And yes, I know that might've been a bit cheesy, but something about literally covering myself up in that mirror made everything click for me. Now, every day as I get up from my bed, I see Jesus. I see a reminder of humility about who I am, compared to who He is and the sacrifice that He made for me. And honestly, by seeing Jesus instead of myself in my mirror every day, I've noticed I am becoming less worried about how I look or if my outfit looks good. Now I focus more on whether my inside looks good, and if my heart is clothed with Jesus's love as I walk out my door.

All this to say, to have more of Jesus in your life, there *has to be* less of you. But that doesn't mean you must become nothing, or that you aren't significant or of value. It doesn't mean you are literally dying to yourself to get rid of who you are. It simply means you are dying to the *part of you* that's selfish and wants to live for itself. It means your desire to make your name known is going down, because you're realizing it's God's name that should be going up. That's what it means to have humility in Jesus—knowing who you are compared to who He is, and realizing it's far more important to make His name known than yours. It's not that you aren't important, it's that God is infinitely more important. And so, you have to be willing to give up the parts of you that desire fame, attention, and admiration for yourself, to want those things for Jesus.

Often, it's not easy. We want to check ourselves out in the mirror and see how amazing and beautiful we are. We want to make a name for ourselves and be famous in the eyes of people, but Jesus calls us to humble ourselves. Jesus calls us to drop everything and follow

Him. He wants to be our everything. That's the cost of following Jesus, but I promise you, there is so much freedom in that. There is freedom in acknowledging your brokenness to God's goodness and declaring to yourself that God's name is more important than your own.

Don't invalidate yourself, glorify God

Now, I want to stress that making God your everything does not make you nothing. Making God bigger in your life and making yourself smaller does not decrease your value or worth in any way. Yes, it decreases your desire to live for yourself and be your own god, but never should you feel like you must become nothing for God to become everything, because that's just not true.

God created you intentionally and purposefully, with certain gifts, your personality, and talents that set you apart from everybody else in this world. So, if God took the time to handcraft and design you so carefully, why would He ever want you to think you are nothing, or have you give up who you are? Sometimes, we think making ourselves nothing to make God our everything is how God would be most glorified, and we the most humbled. But let me ask you this: How can we be glorifying God when we are invalidating and hiding the unique person that God created to carry out that exact task?

My point is, humbling ourselves before Jesus is not to cancel or invalidate us, but to glorify God. To glorify

God, we must confidently embrace the gifts and the person God made us to be, so we can use these things to make His name known to the world. That's the humble thing to do, ironic as it sounds. God wants us to be confident in the worthy, valuable, and beautiful person He made us to be. He wants us to recognize the gifts He gave us and not just acknowledge them, but use them for Him. Humility before God isn't hiding who we are and hiding the gifts He gave us. It's being confident in those gifts, but knowing they are to point to God to bring glory to His name.

It sounds kind of ironic, doesn't it? That being humble before *God* requires us to be confident about who *we* are? That making God's name bigger requires using your name and your God-given gifts? I think that goes to show another way the Kingdom of God is truly upside down. You would expect, that to be humbled to the King of the Universe would mean we would have to be made nothing. You would expect we should never go around sharing about ourselves and our gifts. You would expect we would pretty much all be robots who are all the same, and just give glory to His name.

But that's not how it is. God loved us too much to make us all robots. In fact, He loved us so much that He took the time to intentionally design each one of us and give each of us unique gifts. He made it so that we would *have* to love and value ourselves for us to be confident in using and sharing those gifts with the world, for the sake of His Kingdom. He made it so that in order to glorify Him, we would *have* to recognize our uniqueness and specialness, and realize what we offer is so important. Unlike robots, which are all the same so that it doesn't matter whether one robot is missing, God made all His creations vital to the body of Christ and its mission. It says in 1 Corinthians 12:14–20:

"For the body does not consist of one member but of many. If the foot should say, 'Because I am not a hand, I do not belong to the body,' that would not make it any less a part of the body. And if the ear should say, 'Because I am not an eye, I do not belong to the body,' that would not make it any less a part of the body. If the whole body were an eye, where would be the sense of hearing? If the whole body were an ear, where would be the sense of smell? But as it is, God arranged the members in the body, each one of them, as he chose."

In other words, God made each of us have a role and purpose in carrying out His kingdom here on earth. Each of us are a vital part in bringing God glory. Therefore, in humility and obedience to God, we must recognize Christ is the head of the body. He is infinitely important, but He made us a part of the body, which gives us an important role in supporting the head.

Your unique cup
I wanted to end this chapter with an analogy that my mentor, Pastor Esther, once told me: Every single one of us is like a cup God specially and intentionally designed. God gave each one of us unique gifts,

personality traits, and talents that set us apart from everybody else.

But a lot of the time, we try to hide these gifts we've been given. We try to cover up all our uniqueness and everything that makes us special by coloring our cups to be just a solid color to be like everybody else (like robots!). We think it would be "arrogant" or "not humble" to go out into the world and show people our gifts and talents, so we try to hide them. We keep them to ourselves, thinking that's what humility is.

Except we aren't called to follow the world's definition of humility, which makes us feel like we must deny what we're good at and make people think we're less than we really are. We are called to follow God's definition of humility, and His definition says our gifts and talents were given to us *on purpose* and *for purpose*. They are to bless others, encourage others, and point people to Christ. God didn't create us to be solid-colored cups, but to be the intricate and beautifully designed cups He planned us to be long before He created us. So, it's humble to be confident in our gifts. I mean, that's the best thing we could do as God's creations, right? To be obedient and to embrace what God has given us and use what we've been given to glorify Him and His kingdom. I believe that's the humbleness we are called to have.

To recognize God is higher than us and is our Maker, and that it's more prideful and arrogant when we want to keep our gifts to ourselves. That it's arrogant for us to hide our talents out of fear because we are trying to gain approval from people instead of from God. I believe it's in humility that we must go out and share our gifts with the world. Whether that's leading praise at church because God gave you the gift of singing, or whether it's running for class president because God gave you a heart to love your peers, we are each called to use our gifts for God's kingdom. Let's all be humble in this way and be the beautiful cups that God has designed us *all* to be!

8

Finding Me

"How did you find yourself through finding God?"

Even before I found God, I was still His child. Even before I met Him, I was still deeply loved by Him, and even before God gave life to me, He sent His Son to die for me. Before I found God, I was still His masterpiece, His precious creation, and His beloved daughter. I was all these things to God even before I recognized, acknowledged, or accepted Him into my life. God created me, therefore He knew exactly who I was even when I didn't have a clue.

That's why this book is called *Finding God, Finding Me*. God already knew who I was, so when I found Him, I found who I was through who He already knew and believed me to be. It wasn't me magically becoming someone else entirely when I met God, but rather, it was me discovering and realizing who God made me to be all along. I was always God's child. I was always His masterpiece, His beautiful creation. And I was always deeply and unconditionally loved by Him. *I just had to realize it.*

Each of the past six chapters started with a lie I had believed about myself. In the identity chapter, I believed the lie that I had to prove my worth and value through the sport I played. In the confidence chapter, I believed the lie that there was nothing good enough in me to feel secure. In the patience chapter, I believed I couldn't help my irritability; in the purpose chapter, I believed my motivation should be to be praised by the world; in the passion chapter, I believed I was simply a slave to passivity, and finally, in the humility chapter, I believed everything revolved around me.

All these lies I believed to be true about myself and my life covered up the fearfully and wonderfully made daughter God created me to be. These lies prevented me from seeing who I truly was and who God had set me apart to be from the beginning. Instead of seeing myself through the lens of God's truth, I saw myself through the lens of the devil's lies. Through that lens, I was simply a slave—to volleyball, insecurity, irritability, selfishness, passivity, and pride.

I had to find God and find out who He saw me as to find who I truly was in Him. I had to let God's truth tear down and replace the lies that covered up my true worth and identity. I had to allow God to break off all the chains holding me back and take off all the layers of labels and comments I fell into the trap of believing. It was when all those layers were ripped off that I realized who I was at my core—a child of God who was fully known and deeply loved.

That truth set me free. It set me free to become a new creation. It set me free to be confident in who God made me to be. It set me free to *be me*.

Finding me

As I write this chapter and reflect on the person I am since I've found God, my jaw drops and my eyes widen with incredulity at the transforming power God's truth can have on a life. Before I found God, I saw myself simply as a shy, closed-off, and insecure teenager, but those are no longer the words I use to describe myself. I have been set free from those chains. Through God, I have come to know the truth about who I am. I have found *me*.

I have found the me who loves people with an overflowing love. The me who makes sure everyone feels welcomed, included, and accepted. The me who sees the girl sitting by herself at lunch and goes to sit with her. The me who boldly tells people the gospel as I walk down the street. The me who goes overboard with people's birthdays, because I want people to feel celebrated and cherished. The me who smiles and laughs in every moment I get. The me who puts both hands up in worship. The me who isn't afraid to pursue my dreams that seem too big because of the God I believe in who's bigger. The me who so badly wants to see my generation saved. The me who risks my reputation and people liking me for the sake of making Christ's name known to the world. The me who is willing to drop everything and follow Jesus. The me who loves to sit by the water and dream about the possibility of what God can do through my life. The me who likes nothing more than to sit in a coffee shop with my Bible and highlighters at hand. The me who always carries a journal in case God puts something on my heart to write. The me who wakes up randomly at two in the morning to write a praise song. The me who has absolutely fallen in love with Jesus.

This is the me I have found through finding God. It's the me who is the result of being set free and transformed by realizing His truth. Nothing I wrote above about who I am could exist without Jesus and what He has done in my life. It's the me who's only possible because of Him.

Now, every single morning when I wake up, I choose to be the me that I wrote about above—the me Jesus changed. Every day, I choose not to let the world's standards and the words of other people tell me who I am or decide who I will be. Every day, I choose to not look for my identity in things that aren't lasting and give my life to things bound to fail me.

Loneliness. Emptiness. Depression. Anxiety. Bitterness. Resentment. I choose to not let these words define who I am. And the reason I say all these things are a *choice* is that just because I don't let those words define who I am doesn't mean those words are no longer present in my life. It's a choice I have to make every day, because things like loneliness and emptiness still exist in my life. I would be lying if I told you I don't still struggle sometimes, and feel tempted to go astray.

While Jesus has radically transformed my life, and I *have* found my true self through Him, part of that true self *includes* the me who still feels depressed at times. The me who still questions if my life is being purposeful and meaningful. The me who sometimes forgets the love God showed me the day He changed me. The me who wakes up some mornings and says I'm too tired to read the Bible. The me who sometimes neglects to pray because I say I'm too "busy". The me who still gets hurt by what some people say of me. The me who sometimes looks in the mirror and doesn't like what I see. The me who still gets scared when I do something out of my comfort zone. The me who still gets impatient with my sisters at times. The me who sometimes tries to conform to the world instead of standing firm in who God made me to be. The me who still gets lazy and wastes a lot of my days. The me who's sometimes hard to love.

This is the sinner part of me, and without Jesus in my life, this part of me would be the only part of me. It's only because of Jesus that I have found a new me that I get to choose to be every single day of my life—the me Jesus changed. Every single day, I choose to believe I'm a child of God, and that I've been set free from my sin, guilt, and shame. Every single day, I choose to declare over my life that my sin no longer defines me—all because of Jesus and the price He paid for me.

And so yes, I still struggle. And yes, I still worry, get lazy, impatient, and sin, but because of Jesus, those things do not define who I am—Jesus does. And it was through coming to the acceptance and realization of the truth that *my sin doesn't define me but Jesus does,* that I found the *me* I could be in *Him.*

And let me tell you, the *me I am in Him,* who I choose to be every day, is the me that I am proud of and confident in. That's the me who said yes to writing this book. That's the me who I have found, and it's the me who's only possible because of Jesus.

A perfect ending

Throughout writing this book, God has taken me on such a journey. It started back in the chapter, "Finding God," as I reminisced and recalled when I first felt the love of Jesus and how that changed my life. That chapter was easy to write; I simply described that moment and the change that occurred because of it. But as I wrote the following chapters on finding identity all the way to finding humility, I had a harder time trying to connect all my stories and experiences in a way that clearly described what I found in each chapter.

It wasn't until I prayed and sought God for specific guidance about what to write and what people needed to hear that everything came together. As I set aside a week or two to write each chapter, God revealed exactly how I was to write them. With each topic, or discovery, or short-coming I found, He helped me look back at my life in hindsight and realize I learned a lot more than I thought I had at the time. Not only that, in some chapters, God would literally teach me something about the topic I was writing about by placing some kind of trial or experience in my life that would help deepen my understanding. It was as if I was finding myself all over again while writing this book about how I found me.

Since God had always showed up to reveal the connecting pieces I needed to understand before writing each chapter, I figured He would do the same when it came to finally writing "Finding Me." During the week I was going to write this chapter, I continuously went to God and asked Him to show me what to write. I was expectant to receive some sort of idea from God about an experience or example from my life that would help tie everything together in this final chapter. So as the week went by, I prayed and waited and prayed and waited. I wasn't nervous or anxious at first, because I knew God would show up like He had with all the other chapters, but as the deadline for this chapter came closer and closer, I got worried. I only had a few days left to finish this chapter, and I had barely written anything.

Eventually, Tuesday night of this week came, and my chapter was due in just two days. In frustration, I lied on my bed, looked up at the ceiling, and thought of what I could possibly write that would not only wrap up the chapters in this book, but also the events of my life as adequately as possible. Since I hadn't received or heard anything from God that week, I tried to come up with something by myself. I'll save you the details of all my horrible ideas and just tell you that I probably spent four hours in my bed staring at the ceiling and ending up with nothing of substance.

Finally, it was midnight and I decided I should just sleep. That night, I was having a sleepover with my sister, Olivia, so she was in the bed next to me. In frustration and tiredness, I told my sister I couldn't stay up late talking and said I just needed to go to bed. But as I closed my eyes and drifted off to sleep, my phone vibrated, signaling a text message. I picked up my phone and saw a message that read, "Hey, Izzy, how are you?" When I looked to see who sent it to me, I realized it was from a friend from a really long time ago. I used to play volleyball with this girl, but I hadn't talked to her for over two years.

Confused as to why she was suddenly reaching out to me at well past midnight, I turned my phone off and told myself I would reply the next day. But as I lied in my bed and tried to sleep again, an unsettled feeling rolled over me, and a billion different thoughts ran through my mind. *Was she okay? Why would she be texting me now? Maybe something happened?* Eventually, I decided

I should reply right then and there. Why wait when something might actually be going on?

So, with tired eyes, I picked up my phone and replied, "Hey! Haven't talked to you in a while! I'm doing good, how are you doing?" I barely put my phone back down before it vibrated again with another text message from my friend. She said, "I've been okay. Hey, I know this is really random, but do you think we could meet up? I need to talk to someone about something, and you seemed like just the right person." As soon as I read that message, I quickly sat up from my bed and with full focus and alertness and texted her back saying, "Of course! I'm free to meet up whenever. I'm here for you, hang in there." After I sent that, we scheduled to meet the following day to talk.

After I finished texting her, I put down my phone and instinctively fell on my knees to pray. I didn't know any more details about what was going on, other than she needed someone to talk to, but something in my heart and my spirit told me she was hurting and struggling. So, for a straight ten minutes, I cried out to the Lord to be there for her in that moment. I prayed God would fill her with His comfort, peace, and love, and that she would feel she was not alone. I prayed God would give her strength until the next day when she could talk to me. Whether or not there was actually a serious problem, I prayed like my life depended on it.

When I finished, I hopped back into bed and heard my sister clapping. Laughing because I completely forgot she was sleeping right there next to me, I asked her if she was clapping because of my prayer. But she said that was not why she was clapping. Confused but still laughing, I asked her why she was clapping. And what she said next brought me to tears. She said something no eleven-year-old should have had the profoundness or thoughtfulness to say.

In response to me asking her why she was clapping, she said, "For everything." I asked her what she meant, and she continued by saying, *"just for the person that you are."* My laughter was gone by this point, and I just looked at my sister with tears welling up in my eyes. As we both lay in my bed in complete darkness, I asked her once again what she meant by what she said. After a moment of silence, she went on to say, "Unni (which means sister in Korean), I clapped because of the person that you are. Right after you finished texting that girl you barely knew and that you haven't talked to in years, you fell to your knees praying for her like your life depended on it. Not everyone does that, unni. You're amazing and you inspire me. I'm so proud of you."

With tears in her eyes, she told me some of the most powerful and encouraging words I have ever heard. I didn't know what to say. I just hugged her, and with tears pouring down my eyes as well, I simply told her "I love you, Olivia." And in that moment of sharing tears and vulnerability, everything came full circle for me. To see my little sister, who firsthand witnessed how Jesus changed me from the sister I was to the sister I am today, tell me she was proud of who I was, and say I inspired her, was so humbling and rewarding.

Now, whenever I think about the idea of "finding me," I think back to that moment when Olivia said, "I clapped because of the person that you are," because in the end, I think that's what we all want to hear the most. More than hearing we excel in a particular aspect or become known for a part of our personality, we want to be loved and recognized simply for who we are.

And for me, when Olivia told me those words, it hit me so hard because it reminded me of how Jesus looks at all of us. When He sees us, He sees who we are as a whole. He doesn't just look at the broken part of us and see us as a sinner, and He also doesn't just look at the part of us that's now bursting with confidence and passion in Him. To say we are just a sinner is to discount what Jesus has done in our lives, and to say we are just confident and passionate people is to discount the change that had to happen. God looks at *all* of us, the good, the bad, and the broken, and yet, He still claps in heaven saying, "I'm clapping because of the person I created you to be."

The person God made you to be includes you at the beginning of your journey and you wherever you are in your journey now. And the thing is, you at the beginning of your journey is so important because it has either led to the changed you through Jesus Christ, or because it will lead you to the person you will find yourself to be one day.

When Olivia told me she was proud of the person I was, she was not just patting me on the back because she's now seeing I'm this confident and passionate follower of Jesus. She was clapping because she knew who I was before, and therefore understood my journey to get to who I am now—the person who, in Olivia's eyes, is inspiring.

Final Thoughts

As you've read through the chapters of this book, I hope it has done more than just tell you about my life, but has inspired you to find yours. I think, at first, I was hesitant to write this book because I felt like there was no point in simply sharing about how *I* found God and how *I* found myself and all these other things in the process. I guess I figured a book that literally had the word *me* in the title wouldn't help anybody and simply come across as arrogant.

So, as I started writing this book and sharing about my story and testimony, I felt the pressure of wanting to switch the focus of the book several times to be more about helping to find *you*. As I read other

Christian books and books for teenagers and saw how most of them were all centered around giving tips and messages to help people with very little personal story, I questioned and doubted the helpfulness of my book a lot. I wanted my book to do the same as all these other books and focus on giving advice to help you.

The interesting thing was, during this period of doubt and feeling like I was being too arrogant, I began getting these messages from my friends and people I didn't even know, asking me personal questions—the same questions you saw at the beginning of each chapter. People from my school came up to me asking me things like, "How did you find God?" and "How did you find your identity in Christ?" They asked me how I found my confidence, my passion, and my purpose. These questions came because they saw the way that Jesus had *personally* changed my life. They saw that I was a completely new person, and I believe it was their witnessing of me finding God that led to them asking these questions. They weren't necessarily asking, "How can *I* find confidence?" or even, "How can *I* find God?" They were instead asking me how *I* found these things.

I think we teenagers sometimes hear about this guy named Jesus so often and so abstractly that we never take it seriously or ever really think about it in a deep way. That's why I think it's less impactful when you try to just give people advice or tips on how to find anything, but especially finding Jesus. But when teenagers see their friend, who they relate with and who they love, be changed so radically and dramatically through this Jesus they never thought twice about, they start thinking about it deeper and start taking it seriously.

Ultimately, I've found it was sharing my story and testimony that ended up inspiring and encouraging people the most. It was my friends and the people around me witnessing the change in my life, that made it powerful and impactful enough for them to believe change was possible for them as well. It was my friends seeing this God who had seemed so *distant* to them, radically changing a friend who was so *close* to them, that made God a whole lot more *real* for them.

So, with the encouragement and questions I received from people saying they were inspired to seek Christ because of my changed life, I realized maybe the most powerful thing I could do would be to write a book in response to their questions. I realized maybe I could have the most impact by simply being vulnerable in sharing who I was before, and who I am now because of Christ, and letting this book be a witness and testimony of the power of *Jesus*. And hopefully, by sharing my story, it has inspired and encouraged you to find your story and find hope that Jesus can and will change your life as well.

As I sit here writing the last section of this book, I write to you as a sixteen-year-old girl whose life is probably just like yours. I walk down the school hallways every weekday and stay up late doing homework every night. I'm your typical friend and classmate, and at this point in the book, you basically know everything about me! So, writing to you now as a friend, I'm telling you that my typical and ordinary life got transformed because I encountered Jesus and accepted Him into my life. I was never the type to believe people when they told me God had changed their lives, but here I am, telling you the exact same thing: *God changed my life*. He really did, and if He can change my life, then I have no doubt in my mind that He can change yours.

I believe with all my heart that God placed this book in your hands for a reason. He wants to encounter you and change your life forever, and this book is Him reaching out His hand and telling you to grab hold of it. All the truths about Jesus that I found to be true for my life are also true for you. You are also a child of God, His masterpiece and beautiful creation. And you are also so deeply and unconditionally loved by Him. He knows everything about you, and He loves every part of you. Will you choose to believe that, and find who you are in Him, or will you keep searching for who you are in a world that will keep leaving you feeling empty and unfulfilled?

I can't make you believe God's truth, but I can tell you believing it will change your life. Because when you believe the truth about what God says about you, you will embark on a journey of finding God in your life, and I promise you that you will find yourself in that process. Keep seeking, keep trusting, and keep believing. I'm praying and cheering for you.

> *Ask and it will be given to you; seek and you will find; knock and the door will be opened to you. For everyone who asks receives; the one who seeks finds; and to the one who knocks, the door will be opened* —Matthew 7:7–8

One more thing!

I know you've reached the end of this book, but I believe this is just the beginning—the beginning of TEENAGERS arising and making disciples of all nations, just as Jesus called His people to do.

So, as you put this book down and go on with your life, I want to encourage you to do just one thing: Go and share your testimony with someone in your life, maybe a lot of people in your life. Maybe write a book about it (I'm serious!). If there's anything I've learned while telling people about Jesus, it is that testimonies are so powerful. And what's more powerful is when a teenager shares their story with another teenager.

As much as we need advice and mentorship from the older generation, we also need people our age going through the same struggles as us to teach, lead, and share with us how they found the light at the end of their tunnels, which many times are the tunnels we ourselves are stuck in. We need each other. We need more young people to share. To preach. To witness. And to testify. So, I encourage you to go and share your story and share about Jesus, confidently and unashamed—because our generation needs more of Him.

"Unashamed"
– An original song

*When you told your people to go, I believe that
you meant it
So I will go out and proclaim you without hesitation
For I know that through the words I speak,
you could bring about transformation
And salvation, to every nation.*

*So I will stand unashamed of you
And I will go and do all that you've called me
to do
And I will sing and I will shout out your name
Without a doubt, without a question I will give
you my praise
Cause I'm unashamed*

*So I'll put aside my fear and all my insecurities
So that I can open up to you more possibilities
For I know that if I share your truth, it can set
the people free
Cause I'm sure heaven is where they wanna
be.*

*So I will stand unashamed of you
And I will go and do all that you've called me
to do
And I will sing and I will shout out your name*

Without a doubt, without a question I will give
you my praise
Cause I'm unashamed
Cause I'm unashamed of you
So tell me what to do

I'll go out into the nations
Proclaiming to all of creation
For it's the power of salvation
To all who believe

So I will stand unashamed of you
And I will go and do all that you've called me
to do
And I will sing and I will shout out your name
Without a doubt, without a question I will give
you my praise
Cause I'm unashamed

Let's all be unashamed and change the world for
Jesus:)

ABOUT
KHARIS PUBLISHING

KHARIS PUBLISHING is an independent, traditional publishing house with a core mission to publish impactful books, and channel proceeds into establishing mini-libraries or resource centers for orphanages in developing countries, so these kids will learn to read, dream, and grow. Every time you purchase a book from Kharis Publishing or partner as an author, you are helping give these kids an amazing opportunity to read, dream, and grow. Kharis Publishing is an imprint of Kharis Media LLC. Learn more at https://www.kharispublishing.com.

Acknowledgements

First and foremost, thank you God, for changing me in the radical way You did the night at that retreat, and making me the person I am today. Without Your unconditional love and grace that saved me, I would still be living in my darkness. All praise and glory go to You.

This book would not have been possible without the many people who supported, encouraged, and pushed me along the way. I am beyond thankful for all of you and the love you have shown me.

To my mom, who constantly encouraged me to keep going and never give up. In my hardest and most trying moments, you reassured and affirmed both me and my calling to write this book. Thank you for being my number one supporter and friend.

To my dad, who embodies what it means to love God. Your strong faith, that prompted you to ask me those tough questions about my faith, directed me towards having my own relationship with God. Thank you for your listening ear and willingness to challenge me; I am not the same because of it.

To Olivia, who believed in me before I even believed in myself. Every crying night, burst of frustration, and moment of wanting to give up, you were always there to rebuke the lies in my head and remind me of God's truth. Thank you for your unwavering and selfless love for me.

To Noelle, who prayed every night for this book since the moment I told her I was writing it. This book is a result of your faithful prayers. Thank you for being patient and forgiving toward me in my growth as a sister; You make me want to be better.

To Grandma, for being the epitome of selflessness, and showing me what it means to love Jesus. Your dedication to God and doing everything for His glory has pushed me in my own journey with Him.

To Grandpa, who has been the best supporter in anything I do. Your investment in me and willingness to always help has given me stability and peace in the midst of the chaos of life.

To Pastor Esther, who completely changed my life. From the night at your retreat where I met God, to the day at the coffeeshop where you gave me the idea for this book, to every single weekly call you made time for after that, you have been a foundational and transformative part of my journey. You are my mentor, role-model, and inspiration. I can't thank you enough.

To my best friend, Yuna, who showed me what real, Godly friendship looks like. From the day God divinely brought us together, I knew you were a miracle sent straight from Heaven and the answer to so many of my prayers. Thank you for loving and supporting me so well; My life is richer and more joyful because of you.

To Nathan, for inspiring me with your bold faith. To Solomon, for your constant encouragement in all my pursuits. To William, for being a breath of fresh air in my life. I'm thankful for each of your friendships.

To Mrs. Pam Lagomarsino, who believed in this book and poured so much into making it the best it could be. I'm beyond thankful for your willingness to help me in the editing process and all the kind words you spoke over me.

To Rebekah, for your willingness to help me with all the fun parts of this journey, from the cover picture to the promo video; Your vision and artistry made this book come together perfectly.

To all the amazing people I met through Project Encounter. You all are so on fire for God and are a reminder to me of the power and potential of teenagers to change the world for God's Kingdom.

To my church and youth group, where my faith first started. I couldn't be where I am today without this community.

To Kharis Publishing, who took a chance with my book, even despite me being young and a first-time author. I believe God allowed this partnership to happen and for that, I am forever grateful.

To everyone who has given me their friendship, love, and support not just for this book, but for my life. I am so thankful for every one of you.

To God be all the Glory

About the Author

Izzy Koo is a high school student who has dedicated her life to help lead people to Christ. After encountering God in the summer of her freshman year, she felt a deep calling to use her gift of writing and speaking to spread the name of Jesus to teenagers in particular. Since then, she has started the Project Encounter movement, which has become an international gathering of teenagers online to share testimonies and worship the name of Jesus. Izzy also started a blog based off her book "Finding God, Finding Me", which she hopes to be a continuation of her journey she chronicled in this book. You can find her blog at www.mywaytofindingme.com.

Izzy lives at home with her parents and two younger sisters, Olivia and Noelle. In her free time, she loves to write songs, play volleyball with her friends, and meet new people. Yet in all things, she strives to be the best sister, daughter, and friend she can be to those around her, and continuously seeks ways she can glorify God and expand His Kingdom.

CPSIA information can be obtained
at www.ICGtesting.com
Printed in the USA
BVHW070221260521
608094BV00008B/848

9 781637 460306